Dare to Differentiate

TEACHING PRACTICES THAT WORK

Diane Lapp and Douglas Fisher, Series Editors

Designed specifically for busy teachers who value evidence-based instructional practices, books in this series offer ready-to-implement strategies and tools to promote student engagement, improve teaching and learning across the curriculum, and support the academic growth of all students in our increasingly diverse schools. Written by expert authors with extensive experience in "real-time" classrooms, each concise and accessible volume provides useful explanations and examples to guide instruction, as well as step-by-step methods and reproducible materials, all in a convenient large-size format for ease of photocopying.

35 Strategies for Guiding Readers through Informational Texts
Barbara Moss and Virginia S. Loh

The Effective Teacher's Guide, Second Edition:
50 Ways to Engage Students and Promote Interactive Learning
Nancy Frey

Dare to Differentiate, Third Edition:
Vocabulary Strategies for All Students
Danny Brassell

Dare to Differentiate

Vocabulary Strategies for All Students

Third Edition

Danny Brassell

Series Editors' Note
by Diane Lapp and Douglas Fisher

THE GUILFORD PRESS
New York   London

© 2011 The Guilford Press
A Division of Guilford Publications, Inc.
72 Spring Street, New York, NY 10012
www.guilford.com

Printed in the United States of America

This book is printed on acid-free paper.

Last digit is print number: 9 8 7 6 5 4 3 2 1

Library of Congress Cataloging-in-Publication Data

Brassell, Danny.
   Dare to differentiate : vocabulary strategies for all students / by Danny Brassell.
— 3rd ed.
      p. cm. — (Teaching practices that work)
   Includes bibliographical references and index.
   ISBN 978-1-60918-005-8 (pbk.: alk. paper)
   1. Vocabulary—Study and teaching (Elementary) 2. Word recognition—Study
and teaching (Elementary) I. Title.
   LB1574.5.B73 2011
   372.44—dc22
                                                    2010034830

About the Author

Danny Brassell, PhD, is Professor in the Teacher Education Department at California State University, Dominguez Hills. Dr. Brassell is an experienced classroom teacher who has worked with students ranging from preschoolers to rocket scientists, and he has published numerous articles and books, including *75+ Reading Strategies: Boost Achievement and Build a Life-Long Love of Reading* and *A Baker's Dozen of Lessons Learned from the Teaching Trenches.* A reformed reluctant reader now dedicated to creating passionate readers, Dr. Brassell founded the Lazy Readers' Book Club (*www.lazyreaders.com*), which provides recommendations for "cool short books" for all ages. Using humor, music, and games, his workshops have motivated audiences across the country to create cultures in homes, schools, and businesses that stimulate innovation through widespread reading. Dr. Brassell's website is *www.dannybrassell.com.*

Series Editors' Note

As our schools continue to grow in linguistic, cultural, and socioeconomic diversity, educators are committed to implementing instruction that supports both individual and collective growth within their classrooms. In tandem with teacher commitment, schools recognize the need to support teacher collaboration on issues related to implementing, evaluating, and expanding instruction to ensure that all students will graduate from high school with the skills needed to succeed in the workforce. Through our work with teachers across the country, we've become aware of the need for books that can be used to support professional collaboration by grade level and subject area. With these teachers' questions in mind, we decided that a series of books was needed that modeled "real-time" teaching and learning within classroom instruction. Thus the series *Teaching Practices That Work* was born.

Books in this series are distinguished by offering instructional examples that have been studied and refined within authentic classroom settings. Each book is written by one or more educators who are well connected to everyday classroom instruction. Because the series editors are themselves classroom teachers as well as professors, each instructional suggestion has been closely scrutinized for its validity.

There are so many interesting ways to teach vocabulary such that students really learn the words. When teachers rely on just one way, students get bored and learning suffers. Even worse, when teachers simply assign words for students to learn independently, vocabulary gaps widen. In *Dare to Differentiate, Third Edition: Vocabulary Strategies for All Students*, Danny Brassell has assembled a whole host of ways for students to learn vocabulary that are engaging and fun for both teachers and students. The time-tested ideas that Brassell presents in this new edition have been used in classrooms across the country with positive results.

We invite you into the "real-time" teaching offered in this book and hope you'll find this series useful as you validate and expand your teaching repertoire. And if you have an idea for a book, please contact us!

DIANE LAPP
DOUGLAS FISHER

Preface

Since this is a book about teaching vocabulary, I'd like to share one of my favorite vocabulary words: *penumbra*. Without burdening you with lengthy descriptions from Mr. Webster or Ms. Wikipedia, I offer this humble definition: *penumbra* refers to a shadowy, indefinite, or marginal area. It basically refers to the place between lightness and darkness, and that is precisely where I found myself in November 2002.

It was a month before my marriage and a little over a year since I had earned my doctorate, and I attended the California Reading Association's annual conference in Sacramento. There I presented a stirring talk on the impact of increased literacy materials on the early reading conceptualizations of homeless Latino preschoolers, the focus of my dissertation research for the previous 5 years. An audience of two appreciated my rousing speech, one-page handout, and two overhead slides. I felt completely out of place.

Three doors down from me, I noticed that the editors of *The California Reader* were answering questions about how writers could get articles published in their literacy journal. Those editors, Jim Flood and Diane Lapp, not only provided me with tips and encouragement; they offered me a title for one article and insisted I submit it to them. They published my article on how increased use of read-alouds affected a third-grade classroom's reading habits, and soon after that I got a call from Jim Flood asking me if I'd like to coauthor a book with him on vocabulary strategies.

If that seems like a jump to you, you would be quite right. I was an underling (also known as an "assistant professor") at California State University, Dominguez Hills, in south Los Angeles. I had published few articles, presented at fewer conferences, and had very little to offer Jim Flood, a man who had served on the board of directors for the International Reading Association, written hundreds of books and articles, and edited more journals than I had ever read. Basically, Jim's offer of coauthoring a book was the equivalent of Steven Spielberg asking me to collaborate on a movie.

So Jim and I wrote the first edition of this book, entitled *Vocabulary Strategies Every Teacher Needs to Know*, edited by Diane Lapp and Douglas Fisher. Mind you, I was by no means a "vocabulary expert," but Jim, Diane, and Doug saw in me a passionate teacher who loved finding ways to assist teachers. The three of them even invited me to speak at a summer teachers' conference they hosted at San Diego State University (SDSU), and I nervously accepted. I worked for months on the book and spent just about as much time preparing for my 3-hour talk at SDSU, where I would get to speak after Patricia Cunningham—another "rock star" in the literacy community. Audiences warmly received the book and the talk, and I discovered two things in the process: (1) I think teaching vocabulary is essential to producing better, more confident readers, and (2) I love speaking.

Learning vocabulary is a process, a journey that includes plenty of twists and turns—just like teaching. The route to the third edition of this book has included plenty of twists and turns itself.

Jim Flood passed away a few years ago—way too soon. Shortly afterward, Diane Lapp told me that we had run out of copies of the first edition of the book. She gave me the choice of reprinting the first edition or revising it to form a second edition. While a reprinting sounded appealing, my experiences speaking across the country prompted me to write a second edition.

Since the book's initial publication I have spoken in more than 100 cities throughout the United States and presented a variety of vocabulary teaching strategies that I and other teachers have used successfully in classrooms. Inevitably, at the conclusion of any workshop a bleary-eyed teacher confesses that she has no idea how she can implement my ideas with her students. Her students, she assures me, are different. Her students, she confides, need extra attention. Well, having had the pleasure of teaching a variety of students labeled with special needs, I have learned that all students are different. All students require their own special strategies. All students have "special needs."

While teaching all students in the same way may be easier for teachers (and especially test developers), it is often inadequate in meeting the needs of diverse learners. Howard Gardner (1999) noted that students have "multiple intelligences," an idea supported by Robert Sternberg's belief that teachers need to teach students in a variety of ways (Sternberg, Torff, & Grigorenko, 1998). More recently, Carol Ann Tomlinson (2004) has provided teachers with guidelines for what she calls "differentiated instruction" for students. My goal in the second edition of this book was to encourage teachers to get creative during the dark times of "No Child Left Untested" and provide high-quality instruction that meets the needs of all students.

As a result, I gave the second edition the much niftier title of *Dare to Differentiate: Vocabulary Strategies for All Students*. I modified strategies in the second edition to include suggestions for differentiating instruction, and I added many additional web resources. I have had the good fortune to speak with thousands of teachers over the past few years, and they have provided me with tons of suggestions that I "liberated" (I did not steal their ideas; I liberated them, like all good teachers do). Each strategy has benefited from the experience and practice of teachers and students of all ages. In fact, while the first edition was written for elementary school teachers, I have encountered numerous middle and high school teachers who have adapted strategies from the second edition to meet the needs of their students. I thank all of those teachers across the country for their pivotal feedback.

Last year, The Guilford Press took over publication of this book from my original publisher, Academic Professional Development. Speaking in Minneapolis at the annual conference of the International Reading Association, I met with Guilford's Craig Thomas and discussed ideas for the book you have in your hands. The past two editions were spiral bound—which drove me nuts (I am an organization freak, and I like to see book titles on binders)! Additionally, I have been speaking on vocabulary for several years now, and I wanted the book to include more of the "feel" of my presentations. As a result, you will see that this edition has added "flavor" throughout, including many more of the vocabulary games that audiences seem to enjoy so much.

This book is a living, breathing document. I seem to constantly add ideas to this text. By the time you read it, I fully anticipate that I will be kicking myself for not including 13 other ideas I had. Oh, well—I can always write a fourth edition. My hope is that you will find the ideas in this book to be "fun, meaningful, and memorable" for your students. If you would like to offer some of your own tips, please feel free to e-mail me via my website, *www.dannybrassell.com*. Enjoy the book, and remember: You make a difference every day. Thank you for teaching!

References

Gardner, H. (1999). *Frames of mind: The theory of multiple intelligences*. New York: Basic Books.

Sternberg, R., Torff, B., & Grigorenko, E. (1998). Teaching triarchically improves student achievement. *Journal of Educational Psychology, 90*, 374–384.

Tomlinson, C. A. (2004). *How to differentiate instruction in mixed-ability classrooms* (2nd ed.). Boston: Pearson.

Contents

Introduction		1
Strategy 1	Analogies	9
Strategy 2	Barrier Games	16
Strategy 3	Concept Ladders	21
Strategy 4	Contextual Redefinition	26
Strategy 5	Exclusion Brainstorming	33
Strategy 6	Hierarchical and Linear Arrays	38
Strategy 7	Idioms	44
Strategy 8	Interactive Word Walls	49
Strategy 9	K–W–L Plus	55
Strategy 10	List–Group–Label	61
Strategy 11	Morphemic Analysis	67
Strategy 12	Personal Vocabulary Journals	73
Strategy 13	Possible Sentences	79
Strategy 14	Read-Alouds	84
Strategy 15	Scavenger Hunts	90
Strategy 16	Semantic Feature Analysis	94

Contents

Strategy 17   Semantic Mapping   100

Strategy 18   Student VOC Strategy   105

Strategy 19   Text Talk   112

Strategy 20   Vocabulary Self-Collection Strategy   116

Strategy 21   Vocab-o-grams   123

Strategy 22   Vocabulary Cards (Example/Nonexample)   128

Strategy 23   Word Plays   134

Strategy 24   Word Riddles   138

Strategy 25   Word Sorts   143

            Index   147

Word Play Activities

Neologisms/Sniglets   20

Rebuses   31

Eponyms   43

Hink Pinks, Hinky Pinkies, and Hinkity Pinkities   54

Tom Swiftlies   66

Dittograms   78

Book Talk   89

Pangrams   99

Oxymorons   111

Top Ten Lists   122

Palindromes   133

Dare to Differentiate

Introduction

In a Florida suburb a first-grade teacher introduces her students to a unit on "types of weather conditions" and finds that some of her students cannot grasp what she means by the term *blizzard* because they have never seen one. Three thousand miles away a sixth-grade teacher in southern California complains that because his class consists of many English language learners (ELLs), he spends more time repeating new vocabulary words rather than explaining new concepts. Meanwhile, a teacher in rural Nebraska worries that many of her third graders misuse the terms she introduces.

Every day, classroom teachers from coast to coast face a number of challenges. Schools require teachers to teach a wide range of objectives covering a variety of curricular areas that follow specific and often rigid timelines, and vocabulary instruction is not always a teacher's top priority. Some teachers struggle with determining how to provide students with appropriate contexts for learning new words and concepts. Many teachers wonder how much time is appropriate to spend on explicit vocabulary instruction. Still more teachers express concerns over how best to assess student mastery of vocabulary terms.

Let me provide you with some fast facts, meant to impress your friends at dinner parties. After you read each fact, I'd like you to put an index finger to your chin and gasp, "Oh!"

Did you know that average students learn 3,000 to 4,000 words each year (Nagy, 1988)?

Well, if that's the case, that means even the "dingbat" who graduates last in his class from high school has over 36,000 words in his working vocabulary. Where did he learn all those words? Context is everything. While this book provides a number of strategies that show the importance of contextualizing new vocabulary words, an easy way I like to demonstrate this concept to audiences is to examine the role of *context cues* or *context clues* in students' vocabulary development (feel free to use whichever term you prefer, as I have heard educators interchange the two freely). See whether you can determine the meanings of the "nonsense" words below:

Context Cues

poliath:

Tyson hates Fridays because his teacher always gives his class a poliath.

wamzerger:

The other day I was at the mall when I saw a clown playing with a wamzerger. The wamzerger was bright blue and floated above his head. He attached his wamzerger to a string and tied it around his wrist so he would not lose it. The clown and I hit the wamzerger back and forth until my mom told me to come with her.

cacojar:

The cacojar is down the street from Valerie's house. Sometimes she goes to the cacojar with her mother. There are always lots of people standing in line, and the cacojar workers take a long time helping people. Valerie's mom says she would rather not go to the cacojar, but she needs to buy stamps.

If you guessed that the word *poliath* refers to a test, you would be correct. What words helped you come to that understanding? I bet that words such as *Fridays*, *hates*, and *teacher* all evoked prior experiences and background knowledge that led you to determine that a *poliath* is a test.

Did you guess that a *wamzerger* is a balloon? If you did (and you would be correct), which sentence gave it away? I bet that by the time you finished reading the second sentence, you were confident that a *wamzerger* was a balloon. In the first sentence the word *clown* stimulated your brain to picture a clown, but it was probably the word *floated* in the second sentence that allowed you to decide with certainty that a *wamzerger* is, in fact, a balloon.

But sometimes it takes a person a little bit longer to grasp what a new term means, like with *cacojar*. Even though you saw the word four times, you probably did not know for sure that a *cacojar* is a post office until you read the word *stamps*. The combination of your background knowledge and meaningful experiences eventually helped you to determine the word's meaning.

Why do I show students this exercise? (By the way, with young children I use real vocabulary words; I cannot demonstrate this concept as effectively with adults using real vocabulary words, as most adults have developed quite sophisticated vocabularies.) I once attended an "expert's" workshop on teaching students vocabulary, and this "expert" said that average human beings need only to see a word 18 times before they know it forever. When experts rattle off random numbers like that, the first word to pop into my melon is *idiot*. From where did that expert pull that number? The expert's statement reminded me of an old commercial I enjoyed on television as a child, where a boy asked an owl, "How many licks does it take to get to the Tootsie Roll in a Tootsie Roll pop?" The owl licked the sucker three times before devouring the entire lollipop. Handing the boy the remaining slurping stick, the owl declares, "Three."

Vocabulary knowledge has very little to do with the amount of exposures to a word. Rather, what matters most is how meaningful those exposures are. Remember, context is everything. For example, can you remember what you were doing last Tuesday morning? If not, can you remember what you were doing on Tuesday morning, September 11th, 2001? I bet you can remember a lot of details from that day because it was a meaningful experience. I know a word that has been around for a long time, but a lot of people learned it about 5 years ago: *tsunami*. If your name is Katrina and you live in New Orleans, I bet people look at you a little differently since a certain hurricane struck. The way we learn new vocabulary words is through meaningful experiences—context.

Did you know that vocabulary knowledge is one of the best predictors of verbal ability (Jensen, 1980)?

If you took the SAT to get into college, you may have noticed that a large portion of that exam was devoted to word analogies. Why? Well, vocabulary knowledge is a good indicator of how well one will perform in college. Fortunately, test developers have begun to refine their methods of determining students' true vocabulary knowledge, but this will constantly be a topic for thoughtful debate.

Did you know that vocabulary difficulty strongly influences the readability of texts (Klare, 1984)?

Well, this one you may have known. If a student is missing every other word when he or she is reading, that student is probably reading something that is too difficult for him or her. Regardless—are you still putting an index finger to your chin and gasping, "Oh!"?

Finally, did you know that teaching the vocabulary of a selection can improve students' comprehension of the selection (Beck & McKeown, 1983)?

It seems like in every state I visit, the second-grade curriculum of today strongly resembles the fifth-grade curriculum of yesterday. In order to leave no child untested, school districts have felt the pressure of federal mandates. The result has been, as my friend Yvette Zgonc says, a "constipated curriculum": school districts keep adding things for teachers to teach without taking anything away (besides art, music, physical education, field trips, libraries—and anything else that has proven of interest to students). So in the near future when your school district asks you to teach your kindergartners about photosynthesis or the branches of government, it may be a good idea to familiarize students with some key vocabulary before tackling the new subject matter standards.

So, it is well known that vocabulary knowledge is highly correlated with comprehension. After all, students have an easier time understanding texts when they understand the words. Therefore, no matter where they teach, teachers need to understand the importance of enhancing their students' vocabulary knowledge.

The single most important thing a teacher can do to improve students' vocabulary development is to facilitate increased student reading (Cunningham & Stanovich, 1998; Krashen, 2005; Nagy, 1988). Consequently, while it is not explicitly mentioned as a specific strategy in this book, the most important strategy teachers should utilize to enhance their students' vocabulary growth is to provide them with as much time to read for themselves as possible. Teachers should integrate literature into their curricula as much as possible so that students experience words in a variety of contexts. Beyond providing students with high-interest books and time to read them, what are the best ways for teachers to facilitate students' vocabulary growth?

Although research has shown that vocabulary knowledge plays a critical role in students' literacy development, many teachers devote very little class time to vocabulary instruction (Scott, Jamieson-Noel, & Asselin, 2003). Moreover, teachers who do devote time to vocabulary instruction often use strategies that fail to increase students' vocabulary and comprehension abilities (see reviews in Blachowicz & Fisher, 2002; Nagy, 1988). In essence, many teachers seem to either ignore vocabulary instruction or emphasize inefficient approaches.

Think way, way back (some of you further back than others) to when you were a child. How did teachers teach you vocabulary? Next, think about the way you teach vocabulary today. What are the differences, if any, that you can identify?

I'm not sure about you, but when I was a kid, my teachers usually handed us a list of words on Monday morning. The list could range from 20 to 25 words, and teachers expected us to study the words all week in preparation for our vocabulary quiz on Friday mornings. Every now and then I had a teacher who wanted us to practice learning the words by writing sentences with the words. And, smart aleck that I was, I typically tried to use all 20 to 25 words in a single sentence. As an experiment, I'd like you to study the following list of words and then fill out the quiz that follows it.

Monday Morning Words

Study the following words for the next minute (do not take any longer). You may use any study strategy you'd like in order to learn the words:

1. *firkin* (n.)—a small wooden vessel or cask
2. *straddle* (v.)—to walk with legs spread apart
3. *tractable* (adj.)—easily taught; docile
4. *piscatorial* (adj.)—pertaining to fishing
5. *immure* (v.)—to imprison; to shut up in confinement

Friday Morning Quiz

Now, answer the vocabulary questions below:

1. What does *firkin* mean?
2. What does *immure* mean?
3. What does *piscatorial* mean?
4. Now, I will give you the definition, and afterward you write down which word I am referring to: "to walk with legs spread apart."
5. Which word means "easily taught; docile"?

Now, let's grade your quiz. Can you grade your own paper? Look at the "Monday Morning Words" list to see how well you did on your "Friday Morning Quiz." How many words did you define/identify correctly? If you earned a perfect score, good for you. If you got at least one correct, good for you, too.

I actually do not care how well you scored. I am interested mainly in how you studied the words, as I said you could use any study strategy you liked. Did you use the parts of speech to help you out? Perhaps you used word parts to assist you (e.g., for the word *piscatorial*, if you knew the Latin *pisces* refers to fish, that may have helped). Did you orally practice the words with a partner? Did you draw a picture? Did you write a song? All of these strategies are great. Which one is the best? The strategy that works best for you is always the best strategy.

Now, take a moment to look at the following figure:

Q	W	E	R	T	Y	U	I	O	P
A	S	D	F	G	H	J	K	L	
Z	X	C	V	B	N	M			

Does the figure above look familiar? If you guessed that it is the order of letters on the keys of a keyboard, you'd be absolutely right. This order is known as the "QWERTY" configuration, designed by a newspaper editor by the name of C. Latham Sholes in the 1870s. I'm not sure if you have ever heard of things called "typewriters," but they were commonly used in the days before computers so very long ago. If you are familiar with typewriters, you know that each letter of the keyboard had its own "hammer" that typed the letter onto the paper. Secretaries became very good at typing, and often the hammers in their typewriter would jam. They needed a solution to their problem, and so Sholes designed the "QWERTY" configuration—the modern keyboard. Sholes's design intentionally placed the most frequently used letters next to people's weakest fingers. Quite simply, he designed the keyboard in the most inefficient way possible in order to slow typing speed (thus avoiding many "hammer" jams). Since the "QWERTY" keyboard, several alternatives have been introduced, including the "Dvorak" keyboard, which has been shown to be a better ergonomic design and allows people to type much faster. That is why we all use Dvorak keyboards, right? I bet you have never even seen one.

What's my point? I have two points, actually. First, we might be able to effectively cram our short-term memory, but that does not necessarily lead to mastery of concepts in the long term. I know plenty of students (including myself, as a child) who can cram those Monday vocabulary words in their heads, ace the quiz on Friday morning, and promptly forget every one of those words before the start of Saturday-morning cartoons. Second, Monday vocabulary lists and Friday vocabulary quizzes continue to dominate vocabulary instruction. We know they are a waste of time! We know the "QWERTY" configuration is not the best keyboard design. However, we continue to use these tools because we have used them for the past 140 years. That logic reminds me of the vocabulary word *insanity*, which basically means to do the same thing repeatedly and expect a different result.

Fortunately, researchers have learned a great deal about how to teach vocabulary effectively. The teacher who assigns 20 words to her students on Monday so that they can memorize for a quiz on Friday realizes that many, if not all, of her students will forget most of their new terms over the weekend. However, in many classrooms, traditional memorization drills are still used as a primary means of teaching students new vocabulary. This is unfortunate, as Graves and his colleagues (Graves, 2000; Graves & Watts-Taffe, 2002) have advocated broader classroom vocabulary programs for students that (1) facilitate wide reading, (2) teach individual words, (3) provide word-learning strategies, and (4) foster word consciousness.

Since students acquire what they are familiar with, it is critical that teachers expose their students to a variety of different vocabulary-building activities. There is no "one-size-fits-all" program that works everywhere for everyone. Some students respond better to flash cards, while others may prefer collaborative discussions. A healthy vocabulary diet, therefore, includes multiple approaches to accommodate all learners. This book includes a variety of strategies for teachers interested in enhancing their students' vocabulary growth.

Vocabulary instruction is useful in providing students with strategies to use on their own in determining the uses and meanings of unfamiliar words. Teachers who provide vocabulary-building strategies that develop concepts beyond straight definitions give their students a better understanding of how words may be used to apply to their own lives. Students' vocabularies grow gradually, so teachers need to expose students to words used in many different contexts in order for their students to master new word meanings.

Many teachers question which words to teach students. As students acquire an estimated 3,000 to 4,000 words each year (Nagy, 1988), there is no way a teacher can teach every new vocabulary word that students encounter. Teachers may want to look at three primary sources for individual vocabulary words: (1) the new vocabulary introduced in literature that relates to understanding a unit's goals and objectives, (2) basic sight words and high-frequency words, and (3) words found in students' writing.

Finally, many teachers wonder what exactly they should know about word learning and how to create an environment that supports constant student vocabulary interest and understanding. The following list has been suggested (Scott et al., 2003):

1 Word knowledge is complex: Knowing a word is more than knowing a definition.

2 Word learning is incremental: It is a process that involves many small steps.

3 Words are heterogeneous: Different kinds of words require different learning strategies.

4 Definitions, context, and word parts can all supply important information about the meaning of a word, but each of these sources has significant limitations.

The third edition of *Dare to Differentiate: Vocabulary Strategies for All Students* is a collection of strategies based on scientific research designed for classroom teachers interested in providing a variety of vocabulary-learning strategies to their students without sacrificing a large part of time reserved for other curriculum. It is intended to be a "teacher-friendly" resource that teachers can use to provide students with useful strategies toward building stronger vocabularies. This list of strategies is by no means exhaustive. As teachers have consistently used these strategies and achieved positive results with their students, teachers are encouraged to utilize these strategies as a starting point on the road to their students' vocabulary development.

Each strategy is explained in the "What Is It?" and "Why Is It Used?" sections, and procedures for using the strategy are described in the "What Do I Do?" section. Ideas for adapting the strategy to meet the needs of *all* students in your class are given in the "How Do I Differentiate It?" section. The "Example" section describes innovative ways that classroom teachers have utilized the strategy. Curricular goals are listed for each example, and in many cases class-work samples are included. A number of "games" and "tricks of the trade" have been included in this edition. Finally, each strategy concludes with lists of text and web resources and professional references cited in the section. Website domains are constantly changing, and teachers often complain to me that a link I provide no longer works. Here is a great trick I learned from a wonderful speaker, Alan November: Copy the "dead" link (this is any link that says "file not found") and visit the website *www.archive.org.* Paste the link in the site's "Way back Machine," and the site will take you to the old link. So even if a site no longer exists in the present, this Internet "time machine" can take you back to any old site. This tip alone probably just convinced you that this book was worth every penny.

It should also be noted that examples are given for various grade levels, and teachers will always have to adjust their lessons to meet the needs of their students. While the text is designed for elementary school teachers, plenty of middle school and high school teachers have told me how they use the text to accommodate the needs of their students. That does not surprise me in the slightest, as I have used 12th grade strategies with kindergartners, and vice versa (here's a little secret: While 12th-grade strategies do not always work with kindergartners, kindergarten strategies always work with all ages). The goal of this text is to assist teachers in strengthening the ways they teach vocabulary to their students.

References

Beck, I. L., & McKeown, M. G. (1983). Learning words well: A program to teach vocabulary and comprehension. *The Reading Teacher, 36,* 622–625.

Blachowicz, C., & Fisher, P. J. (2002). *Teaching vocabulary in all classrooms* (2nd ed.). Upper Saddle River, NJ: Merrill/Prentice Hall.

Cunningham, A. E., & Stanovich, K. E. (1998). What reading does for the mind. *American Educator* (Spring/Summer), 8–15.

Graves, M. (2000). A vocabulary program to complement and bolster a middle-grade comprehension program. In B. Taylor, M. Graves, & P. van den Broek (Eds.), *Reading for meaning: Fostering comprehension in the middle grades* (pp. 116–135). Newark, DE: International Reading Association.

Graves, M. F., & Watts-Taffe, S. (2002). The place of word consciousness in a research-based vocabulary program. In A. Farstrup & S. J. Samuels (Eds.), *What research has to say about reading instruction* (3rd ed., pp. 140–165). Newark, DE: International Reading Association.

Jensen, A. R. (1980). *Bias in mental testing.* New York: Free Press.

Klare, G. R. (1984). Readability. In P.D. Pearson (Ed.), *Handbook of reading research* (pp. 681–744). New York: Longman.

Krashen, S. (2005). *The power of reading* (2nd ed.). Portsmouth, NH: Heinemann.

Nagy, W. (1988). *Teaching vocabulary to improve reading comprehension.* Newark, DE: International Reading Association.

Scott, J., Jamieson-Noel, D., & Asselin, M. (2003). Vocabulary instruction throughout the school day in 23 Canadian upper-elementary classrooms. *Elementary School Journal, 103*(3), 269–286.

Strategy 1

Analogies

What Is It?

Analogies (Lenski, Wham, & Johns, 1999; Vacca & Vacca, 1995) are used as a way of allowing students to link their prior knowledge with new information. In analogies students have to match two pairs of terms that demonstrate the same relationship. Since analogies require students to draw inferences, they lend themselves well to creative thinking.

Why Is It Used?

The strategy is used to (1) encourage students to attempt various problem-solving techniques to compare two similar relationships, (2) help students to learn to think independently about word relationships, and (3) strengthen conceptual understanding of information.

What Do I Do?

1 Select familiar words from a text. Ask students to explain the relationship that exists between two words. Use different types of analogies (e.g., synonym : antonym, cause : effect, part : whole).

2 Ask students what the relationship is between the two words and explain that analogies are comparisons between two sets of relationships.

3 Allow students to make their own analogies and encourage them to share their analogies with one another. Discuss as a whole class.

4 Show students that analogies have their own symbols (e.g., discover : discovered :: explore : explored). Tell students that the symbol : means "is to" and the symbol :: means "as."

5 Gradually increase the complexity of analogies.

6 Read the text and ask students to highlight unfamiliar words. Discuss new words as a whole class.

7 Develop analogies from a list of new vocabulary words. Encourage students to share their analogies with one another.

How Do I Differentiate It?

Analogies lend themselves to a variety of student-learning modalities. Students can orally practice analogies, visually depict analogies with pictures and flash cards, demonstrate analogies through act-outs, and so on. Ricardo Muñoz uses a variety of free Internet games to encourage his 10th-grade English students to practice analogies. He finds that Readquarium (listed in the website resources), in particular, encourages his class of predominantly English language learners (ELLs) to examine the relationships between different vocabulary words.

Example

Andrew Cohen's fifth graders were studying different explorers who came to the New World. (The unit goals are shown in Figure 1.1.) He asked his students whether they had ever heard of analogies, and a student pointed out that analogies are comparisons that share patterns. When Mr. Cohen asked for an example, the student said that good is to bad as ice cream is to stale milk. Mr. Cohen told the student

---

GRADE 5 SOCIAL STUDIES GOALS

After unit lesson, students will be able to:

1. Describe the entrepreneurial characteristics of early explorers (e.g., Christopher Columbus, Francisco V·squez de Coronado) and the technological developments that made sea exploration by latitude and longitude possible (e.g., compass, sextant, astrolabe, seaworthy ships, chronometers, gunpowder).
2. Explain the aims, obstacles, and accomplishments of the explorers, sponsors, and leaders of key European expeditions and the reasons Europeans chose to explore and colonize the world (e.g., the Spanish Reconquista, the Protestant Reformation, the Counter Reformation).
3. Trace the routes of the major land explorers of the United States, the distances traveled by the explorers, and the Atlantic trade routes that linked Africa, the West Indies, the British colonies, and Europe.
4. Locate on maps of North and South America land claimed by Spain, France, England, Portugal, the Netherlands, Sweden, and Russia.

FIGURE 1.1 Goals for Mr. Cohen's unit on explorers.

that that was a great example of an analogy that followed the "antonym : antonym" pattern. He showed students the book *Explorers Who Got Lost* (Sansevere-Dreher & Renfro, 1994) and selected two words from the text that he was certain the students knew: *Atlantic* and *ocean*. He asked the class whether somebody could make a new analogy, and a student said that *Atlantic* is to *ocean* as *Mississippi* is to *river*. Mr. Cohen asked the class what the relationship was, and students' answers varied from "name : body of water" to "proper name : geographic feature." To ensure that students understood, he used a few more different examples of analogies and asked students to determine the pattern (one student said the lesson was a lot like math, and Mr. Cohen acknowledged that it could be a useful math strategy, too). Then he allowed students to work with partners to create different types of analogies. He asked volunteers to share their analogies. He asked students to read a passage from *Explorers Who Got Lost* and told them to underline words that they did not understand. After students read the passage, Mr. Cohen created a list of all the new vocabulary words and asked students to try to explain what the words meant based on their context. He asked volunteers to come up with a few analogies, and he wrote them on the board. Finally, Mr. Cohen suggested that the students write their own book of analogies to understand their new vocabulary words. He told students to create analogies for all the words and he would include at least one analogy from each set of partners in the class book.

References

Lenski, S. D., Wham, M. A., & Johns, J. L. (1999). *Reading and learning strategies for middle and high school students.* Dubuque, IA: Kendall/Hunt.

Vacca, R. D., & Vacca, J. (1995). *Content area reading* (5th ed.). Glenview, IL: Scott Foresman.

Text Resources

Aaseng, N. (2000). *You are the explorer.* Minneapolis, MN: Oliver Press.

Fritz, J., & Bacon Venti, A. (1994). *Around the world in a hundred years: From Henry the navigator to Magellan.* New York: Putnam.

Gibbons, F., & DuPree, B. (2003). *Hernando DeSoto: A search for good and glory.* New York: John F. Blair.

Goodman, J. E., & McNeely, T. (2001). *Despite all obstacles: LaSalle and the conquest of the Mississippi.* New York: Mikaya Press.

Ross, S. (1996). *Conquerors & explorers.* Brookfield, CT: Copper Beech Books.

Sansevere-Dreher, D., & Renfro, E. (1994). *Explorers who got lost.* New York: Tor Books.

Website Resources

Explorer Links
edtech.kennesaw.edu/web/explorer.html

Kids Online Resources
www.kidsolr.com/history/page2.html

Quia Vocab/Word Knowledge: Awesome Analogies
www.quia.com/cb/7146.html

Readquarium
gamequarium.com/readquarium/vocabulary/analogies/

Sample Analogies

Part I

Directions: Complete each analogy by writing the best word in the blank. An example is given below.

Woman is to man as girl is to __boy__ .

1. December is to winter as March is to _____.
   spring   warmer   parade   autumn

2. Microphone is to in as speaker is to _____.
   sound   out   music   stereo

3. Water is to flood as temperature is to _____.
   hot   degrees   measure   fever

4. Correction is to error as cure is to _____.
   disease   treatment   drug   heal

5. Wheat is to bread as milk is to _____.
   cheese   cow   drink   white

(cont.)

Sample Analogies *(cont.)*

Part II

Directions: Now, build your own analogies.

6.

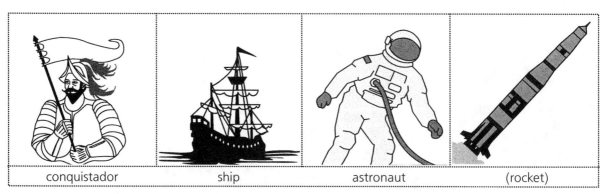

| conquistador | ship | astronaut | (rocket) |

7. explorers : 16th century :: astronauts : _____

8. Christopher Columbus : Isabel I :: Sir Francis Drake : _____

9. longitude : compass :: speed : _____

10. explore : colonize :: seek : _____

Answers: 1. spring   2. out   3. fever   4. disease   5. cheese   6. rocket   7. 20th century
8. Elizabeth I   9. odometer   10. discover

Analogies

Directions: Build your own analogies using words and images.

1.

: :: :

2.

: :: :

3.

: :: :

4.

: :: :

5. _____ is to _____ as _____ is to _____.

6. _____ is to _____ as _____ is to _____.

7. _____ is to _____ as _____ is to _____.

8. _____ is to _____ as _____ is to _____.

9. _____ is to _____ as _____ is to _____.

10. _____ : _____ :: _____ : _____

11. _____ : _____ :: _____ : _____

12. _____ : _____ :: _____ : _____

····················· **Strategy 2** ·····················

Barrier Games

What Is It?

Barrier games (Fagan & Prouty, 1997; Herrell, 1999) are flexible teaching tools used to reinforce students' understanding of new vocabulary words and concepts. The aim of a barrier game is for one student to place/identify selected objects onto a game board while describing to a partner what he or she is doing. The partner follows the instructions to replicate what is being done, sight unseen. At the end of the game the objects should be in identical positions on both game boards.

Why Is It Used?

The strategy is used to (1) elicit students' spontaneous speech, and (2) allow students to practice new vocabulary terms (especially related to a new concept).

What Do I Do?

1 Give pairs of students a screen or board to act as a barrier between them (three sides of a cardboard box can be used effectively) and two identical game boards and sets of identical objects.

2 Ask students to set up their barriers so that they may place and identify the objects on their game boards without being observed by their partner.

3 The first student selects an object and describes it to the partner. The student then places it on the game board, describing the location to the partner.

4 The partner selects the object matching the description from an identical collection and places it on the position that the first student described.

5 The first student continues to describe and place objects until a selection or all objects are placed.

6 The students remove the barrier and compare their arrangements. The object of the game is to match both sides exactly. Tell students to discuss the differences and similarities between their game boards.

How Do I Differentiate It?

Barrier games allow students to explore vocabulary words on their own time. This makes barrier games an optimal teaching tool for teachers, who can create a number of different "barrier-game centers" that introduce or review new vocabulary words to students. Observations of different classrooms have shown that students will use barrier games as a way of practicing words verbally, writing new words in silly stories, and creating improvisational skits that use new terminology. Best of all, barrier games allow word reinforcement without sacrificing instructional time, and many students play barrier games on their own outside of school.

Example

Rima Hossein's third graders were studying fractions and decimals by practicing with money. In this way Ms. Hossein was covering a number of the math objectives. (The unit goals are shown in Figure 2.1.) Her students loved math because Ms. Hossein had created a number of centers that offered students games to play. Students enjoyed barrier games because they had the opportunity to work in pairs. Ms. Hossein had designed different barrier games almost every week, depending on what new concepts she was trying to teach. This week, two of her boys (Victor

---

GRADE 3 MATHEMATICS GOALS

After unit lesson, students will be able to:

1. Compare fractions represented by drawings or concrete materials to show equivalency and to add and subtract simple fractions in context (e.g., 1/2 of a pizza is the same amount as 2/4 of another pizza that is the same size; show that 3/8 is larger than 1/4).

2. Add and subtract simple fractions (e.g., determine that 1/8 + 3/8 is the same as 1/2).

3. Solve problems involving addition, subtraction, multiplication, and division of money amounts in decimal notation and multiply and divide money amounts in decimal notation by using whole-number multipliers and divisors.

4. Know and understand that fractions and decimals are two different representations of the same concept (e.g., 50 cents is 1/2 of a dollar, 75 cents is 3/4 of a dollar).

FIGURE 2.1. Goals of Ms. Hossein's unit on fractions and decimals.

Victor		Manuel	
1/4	♩	1/4	♩
50 cents	🪙🪙	50 cents	🪙🪙
one quarter	🪙🪙🪙	one quarter	🪙🪙🪙
$0.75	75¢	$0.75	$0.75
a dollar	$1.00	a dollar	$1.00
half a dollar	🪙🪙	half a dollar	🪙🪙
seventy-five cents	$0.75	seventy-five cents	75¢

FIGURE 2.2. Student example of a barrier game. Both partners had the same types of items: fake coins, musical notes, decimal cards, fraction cards, dollar/cent cards, and word cards.

and Manuel) played a "money decimals" barrier game at their table (see Figure 2.2). They placed a recycled pizza box between them, and each had an identical game board and bag of items (both partners had the same types of items: fake coins, musical notes, decimal cards, fraction cards, dollar/cent cards, and word cards). Victor chose items to match various spots on the game board and then gave clues to Manuel. For example, for "1/4" Victor said that it was the type of quarter you see when you sing music, and Manuel chose a quarter note from his bag. When they finished their game, they removed their barrier and found that they had almost identical boards. They talked about why Manuel chose to use decimals instead of cents for "0.75" and "seventy-five cents," respectively. While Ms. Hossein had taught them how to play the barrier game, she never had any direct involvement with the two boys as they played the game.

References

Fagan, M., & Prouty, V. (1997). *Language strategies for children: Keys to classroom success.* New York: Thinking Publications.

Herrell, A. L. (1999). *Fifty strategies for teaching English language learners.* Upper Saddle River, NJ: Prentice Hall.

Text Resources

Allen, N. K., & Doyle, A. (1999). *Once upon a dime: A math adventure.* Waterton, MA: Charlesbridge.

Daniels, T., & Bush, T. (2001). *Math man.* New York: Scholastic.

Maestro, B., & Maestro, G. (1993). *The story of money.* Boston: Houghton Mifflin.

Pinczes, E. J., & Enos, R. (2001). *Inchworm and a half.* Boston: Houghton Mifflin.

Thompson, L., & Wingerter, L. S. (2001). *One riddle, one answer.* New York: Scholastic.

Viorst, J., & Cruz, R. (1988). *Alexander, who used to be rich last Sunday.* New York: Aladdin Books.

Website Resources

All About Fractions
www.aaamath.com/fra.html

AplusMath
www.aplusmath.com

Cool Math 4 Kids—Fractions
www.coolmath4kids.com/fractions/index.html

Fun Brain Money Math
www.funbrain.com/cashreg

The Problem Site
www.theproblemsite.com

WORD PLAY:
Neologisms/Sniglets

A neologism is a new word, meaning, usage, or phrase. One way to get students to pay attention to language is to encourage them to play with words. For many years the *Washington Post's* Style Invitational has asked readers to take any word from the dictionary and alter it by adding, subtracting, or changing one letter, and supply a new definition. Comedian Rich Hall (1986) used to encourage people to send him neologisms he called "sniglets," which he defined as "words that are not in the English dictionary but should be." Here are some examples of silly neologisms/sniglets:

1. *aquadextrous*—possessing the ability to turn the bathtub tap on and off with your toes

2. *cashtration*—the act of buying a house, which renders the subject financially impotent for an indefinite period

3. *crackberry*—person addicted to his or her Blackberry device

4. *drainchild*—not all brainchildren work well so we need a word for a bright idea that drains resources without benefit

5. *elbonics*—the actions of two people maneuvering for one armrest in a movie theater

6. *minutater*—the smallest French fry in a pack of McDonald's French fries

7. *phonesia*—the affliction of dialing a phone number and forgetting who you were calling just as he or she answers

8. *politricks*—tool used by politicians

9. *shrub head*—a gardener who smokes the plants after trimming them

10. *telecrastination*—the act of always letting the phone ring at least twice before you pick it up, even when you're only 6 inches away

TEXT RESOURCES

Hall, R. (1986). *Unexplained sniglets of the universe*. New York: Macmillan.
Wallraff, B. (2006). *Word fugitives: In pursuit of wanted words*. New York: Harper.

Concept Ladders

What Is It?

Concept ladders (Gillet & Temple, 1986; Upton, 1973) are used as a way of getting students to focus on one particular word or concept rather than on a set of words. Concept ladders are graphics that use questions in relation to determining exact meanings for concepts. In a concept ladder, the new concept or word appears in the center of the ladder, and students are asked to "climb up" the ladder to determine what the concept or word is and what it is composed of or to "climb down" the ladder to determine examples and uses of the concept or word.

Why Is It Used?

The strategy is used to (1) encourage students to think of the meaning of one word in relation to the meaning of others, and (2) teach important concepts in the concept areas.

What Do I Do?

1   Using the chalkboard or an overhead transparency for a concept ladder, select a key word or concept. Write it on the concept ladder next to "concept/word" (see Figure 3.2 below).

2   Ask students about their understandings of the concept/word. Adjust questions to fit different concepts/words:

   a What is it a kind of/what are kinds of it?

   b What is it a part of/what are parts of it?

ⓒ What is it a stage of/what are stages of it?

ⓓ What is it a product or result of/what are the products or results of it?

3 Tell students to keep a concept ladder in mind when reading text and search for any new concepts or words in their reading.

How Do I Differentiate It?

Synedah Blackman has found that concept ladders work extremely well with the boys in her sixth-grade class, but the girls use concept ladders in an even more imaginative way (supported by research found in Bleach, 1998). Ms. Blackman introduces various newspaper articles (supported in Brassell, 2007) to the class and permits students to further research various concepts found in those articles. She then allows students to report their findings to their classmates in a variety of ways, from video- and audio-recorded news broadcasts to class news critiques and collages.

Example

Tom Shafer's fourth graders were avid writers, and he wanted to make them aware of different types of writing (e.g., informative reports, narratives, responses to literature). The unit goals are shown in Figure 3.1. While his students were aware of what narratives were, he was not convinced that they were fully aware of their various forms and uses. Using the overhead projector, Mr. Shafer drew a concept ladder with the term *narrative* as his key concept. He asked his students to brainstorm everything they knew about narratives and filled in the transparency where he found appropriate (see Figure 3.2). Mr. Shafer asked the students to look for the details that authors provided in their narratives as they read independently, and he asked the class to take that into consideration when they performed their own writing.

GRADE 4 LANGUAGE ARTS GOALS

After unit lesson, students will be able to:

1. Relate ideas, observations, or recollections of an event or experience.
2. Provide a context to enable the reader to imagine the world of the event or experience.
3. Use concrete sensory details.
4. Provide insight into why the selected event or experience is memorable.

FIGURE 3.1. Goals for Mr. Shafer's unit on types of writing.

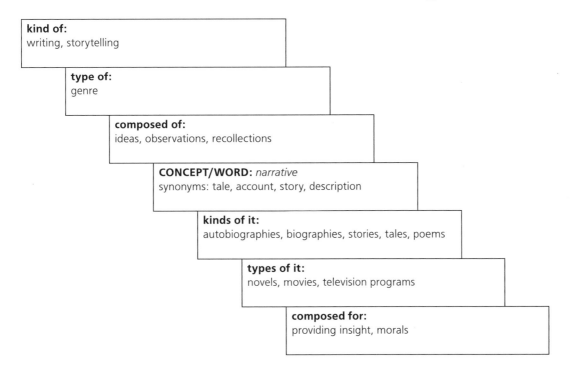

FIGURE 3.2. Example of concept ladder.

References

Bleach, K. (1998). *Raising boys' achievement in schools*. London: Trentham Books.

Brassell, D. (2007). *News flash! Newspaper activities to meet language-arts standards and differentiate instruction*. Peterborough, NH: Crystal Springs.

Gillet, J. W., & Temple, C. (1986). *Understanding reading problems: Assessment and instruction*. Boston: Little, Brown.

Upton, A. (1973). *Design for thinking: A first book on semantics*. Palo Alto, CA: Pacific Press.

Text Resources

Bridges, R. (1999). *Through my eyes*. New York: Scholastic Trade.

Coerr, E., & Himler, R. (1999). *Sadako and the thousand paper cranes*. New York: Puffin.

Craighead George, J., & Cowdrey, R. (1997). *The tarantula in my purse: And 172 other wild pets*. New York: Scott Foresman.

Jimenez, F. (1997). *The circuit*. Albuquerque: University of New Mexico Press.

Snicket, L. (2002). *Lemony Snicket: The unauthorized autobiography*. New York: HarperCollins.

Spinelli, J. (1998). *Knots in my yo-yo string: The autobiography of a kid*. New York: Knopf.

Website Resources

Kids Mysteries
kids.mysterynet.com/writing

Six Word Stories
www.sixwordstories.net

Stone Soup, the magazine by children
www.stonesoup.com

Concept Ladder

kind of:

type of:

composed of:

CONCEPT/WORD: _____

kinds of it:

types of it:

composed for:

Contextual Redefinition

What Is It?

Contextual redefinition (Readence, Bean, & Baldwin, 1995; Tierney, Readence, & Dishner, 1995) is an instructional strategy used to help students acquire the ability to use context and structural analysis to determine the meaning of unfamiliar words. Using contextual redefinition, the teacher models how to figure out the meaning of an unfamiliar word. This is done through structural analyses such as using prefixes, suffixes, and root words to associate with other meaningful word parts.

Why Is It Used?

The strategy is used to (1) demonstrate to students the importance of using all contextual clues available to determine the meaning of unfamiliar words, (2) show students how to make educated guesses about the meanings of unfamiliar words utilizing context, (3) make students active participants in the discovery of new words, and (4) allow students to share their thought processes with one another and understand different ways to derive meaning from print.

What Do I Do?

1 Using a text passage, select unfamiliar words as key words.

2 Write a sentence on the chalkboard or on an overhead transparency that permits students to guess the meaning of the key words through the use of contextual clues. If the text already has such a context, use that one. If an original sentence is required, include various clues such as synonyms or analogies.

3 Using the chalkboard or overhead, show students the words in isolation, pronounce them, and ask them to predict each word's meaning.

4 As students present their definitions for words, ask them to provide a rationale for their thinking. Record definitions given by students.

5 Ask students to look at words in their appropriate context, using the sentences previously presented on the chalkboard or overhead. Again, allow students to present their definitions of the words and to provide a rationale for their thinking.

6 Ask students to reflect on their predictions and revise, if necessary.

7 Tell students to use dictionaries to verify their predictions.

8 Discuss quality of predictions when words are presented in isolation versus in context.

How Do I Differentiate It?

Contextual redefinition allows students to search for context clues embedded in paragraphs to help them learn the meanings of the new target vocabulary words. A good way to differentiate how contextual redefinition is presented to students, according to second-grade teacher Sally Hawkins, is to provide lots of different contexts for students to use their reading skills. For example, too many reluctant readers associate reading with textbooks and exams. Teachers can introduce new target words in comic books, graphic novels, newspaper advertisements, screenplays, and so on.

Example

Gagan Roy told her second graders that they would begin studying fractions. (The unit goals are shown in Figure 4.1.) When a student asked her what fractions were, Ms. Roy said that they would learn together. On the chalkboard she listed five words that she thought the students would be using throughout the week as they read about fractions. She asked them to vote on their knowledge of each word. Students

---

GRADE 2 MATH GOALS

After unit lesson, students will be able to:

1. Recognize fractions from 1/12 to 1/2.
2. Compare fractions from 1/12 to 1/2.
3. Recognize fractions as part of a whole.
4. Know that when all fractional parts are included, the result is equal to the whole.

FIGURE 4.1. Goals for Ms. Roy's unit on fractions.

could say that they knew and used a word, had heard a word before but might not be sure of its meaning, or did not know a word at all. Next, Ms. Roy decided to create her own sentences using the unfamiliar words. She read the sentences to her class and then covered the sentences with butcher paper. She then asked students to look at the five words and predict what each word meant. Students explained why they defined words the way they did. After students came to a consensus about what each word meant, Ms. Roy showed them the sentences again and asked them to use the clues from the sentences to help discover the unfamiliar words' meanings. Students were allowed to change their definitions if they wanted, and then all students had to explain why they changed their definitions or kept their definitions the same. Finally, students checked to see whether their definitions matched the ones presented in their dictionaries. The whole class discussed the accuracy of their predictions and

CONTEXTUAL REDEFINITION

Concept/Key Words: Fraction, Whole, Reduce, Divide, Greater

1. My big brother told me he only wanted a *fraction* of my sandwich, not the *whole* thing.
2. Mom and dad *reduced* the amount of time we watch television in half. We only get to watch television for an hour every night instead of 2 hours.
3. The teacher told us to *divide* into groups of four.
4. Two quarters are *greater* than one quarter. That is why Pedro has more money than Sylvia.

Words	0 = Don't know 1 = Have heard 2 = Know & use	Predicted meaning before reading	Meaning after reading	Context clues
fraction	0	I don't know	part of something	He didn't eat all of the sandwich. He only ate part of it.
whole	1	everybody	all of something	If he wanted the whole sandwich, he would eat all of it.
reduce	0	do over	make less	They took away some of the time to watch television.
divide	1	split up	break up	She wants us to get up and get into small groups.
greater	2	better	more than	If you have more than somebody else, you are greater.

FIGURE 4.2. Example of contextual redefinition.

the differences between guessing the meaning of words in isolation compared to words in context. Figure 4.1 shows the results in Ms. Roy's class.

References

Readence, J. E., Bean, W., & Baldwin, R. S. (1995). *Content area reading: An integrated approach* (5th ed.). Dubuque, IA: Kendall/Hunt.

Tierney, R. J., Readence, J. E., & Dishner, E. K. (1995). *Reading strategies and practices* (4th ed.). Boston: Allyn & Bacon.

Text Resources

Adler, D. (1997). *Fraction fun*. New York: Holiday House.

King, A., & Kenyon, T. (1998). *Making fractions (Math for fun)*. Brookfield, CT: Copper Beech Books.

Leedy, L. (1996). *Fraction action*. New York: Scott Foresman.

Long, L. (2001). *Fabulous fractions: Games and activities that make math easy and fun*. Indianapolis, IN: Wiley.

McMillan, B. (1991). *Eating fractions*. New York: Scholastic.

Website Resources

AAA Math Fractions
aaamath.com

Discovery School
school.discoveryeducation.com/homeworkhelp

Henry's Piksas Game
www.baloneyhenryp.com

Visual Fractions
www.visualfractions.com

Contextual Redefinition

Words	0 = Don't know 1 = Have heard 2 = Know & use	Predicted meaning before reading	Meaning after reading	Context clues

WORD PLAY:
Rebuses

Rebus brain teasers use words or letters in interesting orientations to represent common phrases. Here is a sampling of some fun rebuses (you can find huge caches at the recommended websites below):

1. lonely
   excited
   awed
   dismayed
   eager
   resigned

2. noon good

3. deal DEAL
   DEAL deal
   deal _____
   DEAL deal
   deal DEAL

4. LI1stNE

5. nostrihsruoy

6. mi les

7. wineeee

8. cy cy

9. lodgic

10. 0
    B.A.
    M.A.
    Ph.D.

(cont.)

Answers

1. It's lonely at the top.

2. Good afternoon

3. No big deal

4. First in line

5. Your shirt's on backwards.

6. Miles apart

7. Win with ease

8. Cyclone

9. Flawed logic

10. Three degrees below zero

WEBSITE RESOURCES

Braingle
www.braingle.com/brainteasers
With over 15,000 brain teasers, riddles, logic problems, and mind puzzles submitted and ranked by users, Braingle has the largest collection anywhere on the Internet.

Fun with Words
www.fun-with-words.com/rebus_puzzles.html
This site includes many word picture puzzles with hidden meanings to solve from various pictograms.

Puzzle Soup
www.puzzlesoup.com
Every day, this site posts new fun, witty, and challenging rebus puzzles. Currently, there are 1,471 puzzles available in the archives. Solve theses puzzles by interpreting word color, style, position, and information to reveal the answers. These pictograms can be solved with common phrases, movie titles, song lyrics, and geographic locations, along with 25 other categories.

Exclusion Brainstorming

What Is It?

Exclusion brainstorming (Allen, 1999; Blachowicz & Fisher, 2002) is an instructional strategy used to utilize students' prior knowledge and expand their understanding of a social studies or science topic. As a prereading exercise, the teacher presents a list of words to students, and students determine words that do or do not relate to the topic.

Why Is It Used?

The strategy is used to (1) activate students' prior knowledge about new vocabulary words or key concepts, (2) familiarize students with purpose in reading for key concepts and vocabulary, and (3) refine students' predictive skills.

What Do I Do?

1 Place the title and author of the book and an exclusion brainstorming list of words on the chalkboard or an overhead transparency. The words should be new vocabulary words or words or phrases related to the key concept.

2 Explain to students that they will work in groups of four to identify which words they think will most likely appear in the story and those which will not. Tell groups to mark a line through words that they do not think will appear in the story, and remind them that they will have to be prepared to discuss the reasons for their choices.

3 As an example, conduct a discussion as an entire class about the first word on the list.

4 Provide each group with a handout of the list of words. Within each group, ask pairs to read the story together and look for the words as they read.

5 As students work in groups, circulate and observe students' interactions.

6 After students have read the story and discussed the words with their partners, tell small groups to review the exclusion brainstorming list to see how their choices compared to the actual text.

7 Reconvene as an entire class and share results as a class. Discuss how the exclusion brainstorming activity helped students as they read the story and how they can utilize the strategy on their own.

How Do I Differentiate It?

Exclusion brainstorming has proven to be especially beneficial to students at the beginning of the school year, according to first-grade teacher Amanda Moore. Her students enjoy trying to predict what words they are likely to encounter in particular readings. As a result, this strategy is especially useful for teachers to use in exposing students to multiple genres and various reading materials. Students become more confident in their reading and across other content areas by being able to accurately predict the types of vocabulary terminology they are likely to encounter during a given activity.

Example

Tricia Spears had been teaching her sixth graders about different ancient civilizations when she told the class that they would be studying the culture and contributions of the ancient Romans. The unit goals are shown in Figure 5.1. Before they began reading the book *Growing Up in Ancient Rome* (Corbishley & Molan 1993), one of a series of books the class had been reading about different ancient civilizations, Ms. Spears said she wanted to see what students already knew about ancient Rome. On an overhead transparency, she showed her class an exclusion brainstorming exercise. She told the class that the object of the game was to try to determine which words they would see in their readings about ancient Rome and which words they would not see. She told students that they would work in groups and determine which words did not belong by crossing them out (see Figure 5.2). As an example, she reviewed the first two terms on her list: *Romans* and *Martians*. When students laughed and told her that the story would probably not talk about Martians, Ms. Spears drew a line through *Martians*. She told the class that most of the words would appear in the story, but six or seven words did not belong. She asked each group to divide itself into reading pairs and share their opinions as a group afterward. When all students finished reading and discussing their lists, Ms. Spears led a

> **GRADE 6 HISTORY/SOCIAL SCIENCE GOALS**
>
> After unit lesson, students will be able to:
>
> 1. Identify the location and describe the rise of the Roman Republic, including the importance of such mythical and historical figures as Julius Caesar and Cicero.
> 2. Describe the government of the Roman Republic and its significance (e.g., written constitution and tripartite government, checks and balances, civic duty).
> 3. Identify the location of and the political and geographic reasons for the growth of Roman territories and expansion of the empire, including how the empire fostered economic growth through the use of currency and trade routes.
> 4. Discuss the influence of Julius Caesar and Augustus in Rome's transition from republic to empire.
> 5. Discuss the legacies of Roman art and architecture, technology and science, literature, language, and law.

FIGURE 5.1. Goals of Ms. Spears's unit on ancient Rome.

whole-class discussion on which words they had not encountered while reading. She asked students whether they were surprised by any words they had encountered, and students shared their thoughts about the story.

References

Allen, J. (1999). *Words, words, words.* Portland, ME: Stenhouse.

Blachowicz, C., & Fisher, P. J. (2002). *Teaching vocabulary in all classrooms* (2nd ed.). Upper Saddle River, NJ: Merrill/Prentice Hall.

Book title: *Growing Up in Ancient Rome* by: *M. Corbishley & C. Molan*		
• Romans	• Pantheon	• ~~Dynasty~~
• ~~Martians~~	• ~~pizza~~	• Julius Caesar
• amphitheatre	• Colosseum	• Emperor
• taxes	• gladiators	• ~~stormtroopers~~
• public baths	• ~~wrestlers~~	• Hercules
• republic	• chariot races	• circus
• roads	• ~~Pyramids~~	• aqueducts
• ~~highways~~	• Latin	• ~~spices~~

FIGURE 5.2. Example of students' exclusion brainstorming.

Text Resources

Corbishley, M., & Molan, C. (1993). *Growing up in ancient Rome*. New York: Troll Books.

Dowswell, P., & Tomlins, K. (1998). *The Roman record: Hot news from the swirling mists of time*. Boston: EDC Publications.

James, S., Nichols, N., & Graham, C. (2000). *Ancient Rome*. London: DK.

Roxbee Cox, P., & Spenceley, A. (1994). *Who were the Romans?* Boston: EDC Publications.

Solway, A., & Biesty, S. (2003). *Rome: In spectacular cross section*. New York: Scholastic Trade.

Tingay, G. I., & Marks, A. (1991). *The Romans*. Boston: EDC Publications.

Website Resources

Building Vocabulary with Journey North
www.learner.org/jnorth/tm/tips/Tip0023.html#Games

CyberSleuth Kids
cybersleuth-kids.com/sleuth/History/Ancient_Civilizations/Rome

History for Kids: Ancient Rome
www.historyforkids.org/learn/romans/index.htm

The Roman Empire: Children's Section
www.roman-empire.net/children

WORKSHEET 5.1

Exclusion Brainstorming

Book title: _____ **by:** _____

-
-
-

-
-
-

-
-
-

-
-
-

-
-
-

-
-
-

-
-
-

-
-
-

-
-
-

Hierarchical and Linear Arrays

What Is It?

Hierarchical and linear arrays (Allen, 1999; Nagy, 1988) are additional instructional strategies used to help students understand the relationships between words. Hierarchical arrays use "tree" diagrams that allow students to comprehend the hierarchical relationships between words. Linear arrays use lines to arrange words in order by degree of size, time of occurrence, expense, and so on. How an array is structured depends on the concept(s) being examined. Variations of hierarchical and linear arrays include "concept ladders," (discussed in Strategy 3) "thinking trees," and "semantic gradients."

Why Is It Used?

These strategies are used to (1) allow students to develop concepts, (2) help students learn to think independently about word relationships, and (3) show students how to compare and contrast words.

What Do I Do?

1 Select a key word or concept.

2 Show students the type of array that will be constructed.

3 Using the chalkboard or overhead projector, create an array.

4 As students offer suggestions for words to include in the array, record students' words in their proper position on the array.

5 Discuss the relationship between words as the array is developed.

6 As unit of study progresses, encourage students to add to or change the array.

How Do I Differentiate It?

Hierarchical and linear arrays provide opportunities for students to graphically display their knowledge of different words and how they relate to different concepts. Nadia Rosmanov reports that her ELL students, in particular, appreciate using hierarchical and linear arrays. Too often Mrs. Rosmanov has found that her ELL students are evaluated based on their language skills, not their knowledge. She trains her third graders to demonstrate what they know graphically, and she has found that students often learn new vocabulary target words quicker because of their graphic representations.

Example

Rick Johnson wanted his sixth graders to use the scientific method whenever they needed to answer questions. (The unit goals are shown in Figure 6.1.) First, he wanted to make sure that his students understood what the scientific method was, so he asked them to form into groups of five. He had each group of students hold the hands of two people across from them and then asked students to untangle themselves without letting go of their two partners' hands. After all of the groups managed to untangle themselves with varying degrees of success, Mr. Johnson asked the class to review the steps they used to solve the problem. He listed these steps as the scientific method of inquiry on the chalkboard by creating a linear array (students developed hypotheses—tested their hypotheses—evaluated their data—developed new questions). Mr. Johnson told the class that they had created a linear array to better understand the scientific method. Next, he asked students whether any questions they asked themselves were more important than others. By organizing these

---

GRADE 6 SCIENCE GOALS

After unit lesson, students will be able to:

1. Develop their own questions and perform investigations.
2. Develop a hypothesis.
3. Test their hypothesis by collecting data.
4. Evaluate their data.
5. Develop new questions.

FIGURE 6.1. Goals for Mr. Johnson's unit on the scientific method.

Linear Array: "The Scientific Method"
question → develop hypothesis → test hypothesis → collect data →
evaluate data → develop new questions

Hierarchical Array: Most Important Steps in Answering Question

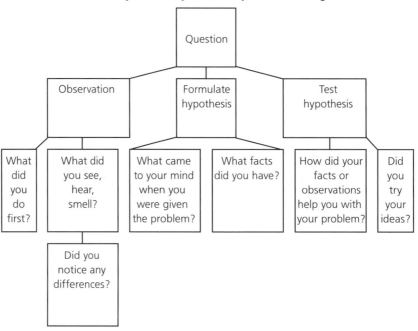

FIGURE 6.2. Examples of linear and hierarchical arrays.

questions in order of importance, the class was able to create a hierarchical array. The class discussed the relationships between various words and/or concepts. Mr. Johnson encouraged his students to add to the arrays when they saw fit as they practiced using the scientific method. Figure 6.2 shows the linear and hierarchical arrays created by is class.

References

Allen, J. (1999). *Words, words, words*. Portland, ME: Stenhouse.
Nagy, W. (1988). *Teaching vocabulary to improve reading comprehension*. Newark, DE: International Reading Association.

Text Resources

Freedman, R. (1994). *The Wright brothers: How they invented the airplane*. New York: Holiday House.
Freiberger, P. (1999). *Fire in the valley: The making of the personal computer*. Boston: McGraw-Hill Trade.

Jones, C. F. (1998). *Accidents may happen: Fifty inventions discovered by mistake.* New York: Random House.

Macaulay, D. (1979). *Motel of the mysteries.* Boston: Houghton Mifflin.

Roberts, R. (1989). *Serendipity: Accidental discoveries in science.* Indianapolis, IN: Wiley.

Tucker, T. (1998). *Brainstorm: The stories of twenty American kid inventors.* Geneva, IL: Sunburst.

Website Resources

Pictograms
   pbskids.org/sagwa/games/picturesaswords/index.html

Rebus Puzzles
   www.fun-with-words.com/rebus_puzzles.html

The Scientific Method
   www.visionlearning.com/

The Scientific Method Today
   www.scientificmethod.com/

Teaching the Scientific Method
   sciencefairproject.virtualave.net/teacher_resources.htm

Linear and Hierarchical Arrays

HIERARCHICAL ARRAY

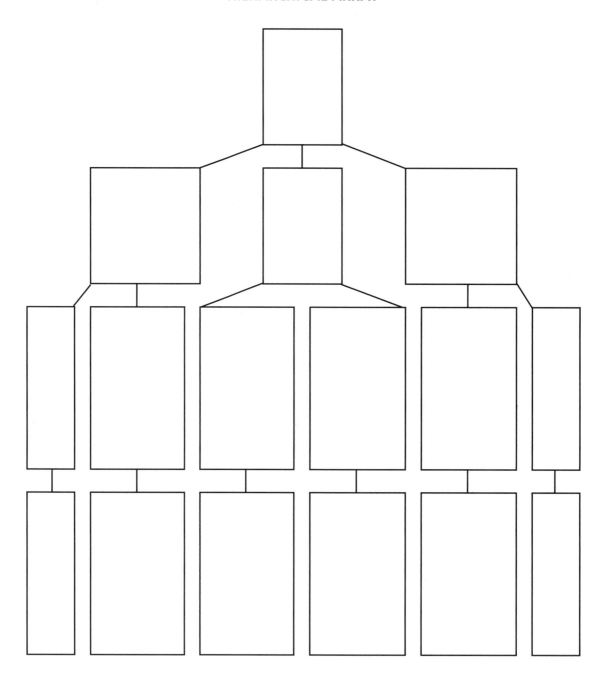

LINEAR ARRAY

WORD PLAY:
Eponyms

An eponym is a general term used to describe from what or whom something derived its name. Eponyms may be derived from the name of a real, fictional, mythical, or spurious character or person, or even a product. Ask students to search for everyday eponyms they may hear or see. Here are some examples:

"People" Eponyms

asphalt—Leopold von Asphalt (1802–1880), Bavarian landowner

diesel—Rudolf Diesel (1858–1913), German mechanical engineer

flora—Flora, Roman goddess of flowers, youth, and spring

jumbo—Jumbo, 62–ton African elephant exhibited at London Zoo from 1865 to 1882

maverick—Samuel Augustus Maverick (1803–1870), American pioneer

Pennsylvania—Sir William Penn (1621–1670), British admiral

teddy bear—Theodore Roosevelt (1858–1919), American president

Uzi—Uziel Gal (1923–2002), Israeli inventor

Zany—Zanni, traditional masked clown in the Italian commedia dell'arte

"Product" Eponyms

Band-Aid—Johnson & Johnson, plastic adhesive bandage strip

Escalator—Otis Elevator Company, power-driven stair system

Jell-O—Kraft Foods, Inc., fruit-flavored gelatin

Kleenex—Kimberly-Clark Corporation, soft facial tissue

Kool-Aid—Kraft Foods, Inc., instant lemonade/soft-drink mix

Popsicle—Good Humor—Breyers Ice Cream Company, colored ice candy on a stick

Scotch tape—Minnesota Mining and Manufacturing Company (3M), cellophane adhesive tape

Styrofoam—Dow Chemical Company, extruded polystyrene insulating foam

Wite-Out—BIC Corporation, correction fluid

Xerox—Xerox Corporation, photocopy machines

WEBSITE RESOURCE

Eponym Practice
users.tinyonline.co.uk/gswithenbank/eponyms.htm

There are thousands of eponyms in everyday use in English today, and the study of them yields a fascinating insight into the rich heritage of English and its development. This site includes numerous examples of names that have been immortalized in such a way.

Idioms

What Is It?

Idioms (Blachowicz & Fisher, 2002; Fernando, 1996) are types of expressions whose meanings cannot be predicted from the usual meanings of their parts. Since students frequently encounter idiomatic expressions in spoken and written discourse, teaching idioms is a useful strategy in exposing students to the meanings of such phrases.

Why Is It Used?

The strategy is used to (1) familiarize students with frequent expressions that cannot be defined by their literal meanings, (2) allow students to realize the absurdity of idiomatic expressions' literal meanings and provide links from the literal words to the nonliteral meanings, and (3) show students why figurative language is used in writing.

What Do I Do?

1 From a text select some idiomatic expressions (e.g., the test was a piece of cake).

2 Write the idiomatic expression on the chalkboard or on an overhead transparency. Ask students to draw a picture that illustrates the expression.

3 Ask students to share their pictures.

4 Once students have shared pictures, ask them to predict what the expression means. Write various predictions on the chalkboard or on the overhead transparency.

5 Read a passage from a text that uses idiomatic expression. Allow students to revise their definitions (if necessary) based on the expression's use in the text and then write their own sentence that uses the expressions.

6 Discuss how students were able to determine the meaning of the idiomatic expression from the context of the passage.

7 Write down three to five additional idiomatic expressions from text. Ask students to repeat the steps from before: draw a picture of the expression, predict the expression's meaning, read the text, revise (if necessary) their definitions of each expression, and write their own sentences using each expression.

How Do I Differentiate It?

Hiroku Osa swears that the toughest vocabulary concept for her fourth graders to comprehend is the idiom, as idiomatic expressions require a lot of explaining. Additionally, idioms prove to be confusing to her students, many of whom have emigrated to America from different countries. With so many different cultures to deal with, Mrs. Osa allows students to work in partners and small groups to decipher the meanings of different idioms. She then allows them to demonstrate their understandings in whatever ways they prefer, from pictures to skits, self-authored stories to greeting cards. Idioms lend themselves to a wide variety of differentiated products.

Example

Diana LaFontaine was teaching her fourth graders about various figures of speech and decided to integrate her lesson with their health unit on foods in the food pyramid. (The unit goals are shown in Figure 7.1.) To make the lesson more fun for her students, Ms. LaFontaine told the class that many types of food are used in idiomatic expressions. She showed her students the cover of the book *Who Ordered the Jumbo Shrimp?* (Agee, 1998) and pointed to the author's picture of a jumbo shrimp. She asked the class whether they could guess the meaning of the expression *jumbo shrimp*, and she wrote students' responses on the chalkboard. Ms. LaFontaine read a passage from the story that used the expression and asked her students whether they understood the meaning of the term. She asked students to speak with partners and create their own sentences with the term *jumbo shrimp*, and then the class shared their sentences. She wrote some more idiomatic expressions on the chalkboard and asked students to draw literally what each expression meant and then guess what each expression might mean in the story. Students read the text and revised their definitions if they were incorrect. Students wrote their own sentences with the idiomatic expressions and shared them as a class (see Figure 7.2). Finally, Ms. LaFontaine asked students to think of as many idiomatic expressions that they

---

GRADE 4 LANGUAGE ARTS/HEALTH GOALS

After unit lesson, students will be able to:

1. Apply knowledge of word origins, derivations, synonyms, antonyms, and idioms to determine the meaning of words and phrases.
2. Identify how language usages (e.g., sayings, expressions) reflect regions and cultures.
3. Identify basic health and hygiene practices that benefit overall personal health.
4. Compare their food intake to the recommendations of the USDA Food Guide Pyramid.

FIGURE 7.1. Goals for Ms. LaFontaine's unit on figures of speech.

Pictures			Expression	Definition/Example
	+		= as alike as two peas in a pod	to be very similar; nearly the same *Juan and his brother are as alike as two peas in a pod.*
	+		= to be the apple of someone's eye	to be the person who someone loves most and is very proud of *Even though Maria has two sisters, she is the apple of her mother's eye.*
	+		= as cool as a cucumber	to be very calm and relaxed, especially in a difficult situation *The basketball player was as cool as a cucumber when he took the winning shot.*
	+		= a piece of cake	to be very easy *The test was a piece of cake.*

FIGURE 7.2. Example of student work on idioms.

knew and create a class dictionary of idiomatic expressions. She told students to try, in particular, to think of idiomatic expressions that used food, and she announced that she would give them extra time for reading if they could classify their food expressions into the various food groups of the food pyramid.

References

Blachowicz, C., & Fisher, P. J. (2002). *Teaching vocabulary in all classrooms* (2nd ed.). Upper Saddle River, NJ: Merrill Prentice Hall.

Fernando, C. (1996). *Idioms and idiomaticity.* Oxford, UK: Oxford University Press.

Text Resources

Agee, J. (1998). *Who ordered the jumbo shrimp?* New York: HarperCollins.

Arnold, T. (2001). *More parts.* New York: Dial.

Gwynne, F. (1987). *Chocolate moose for dinner.* Upper Saddle River, NJ: Prentice Hall.

Rosen, M. (1995). *Walking the bridge of your nose: Wordplay poems and rhymes.* Las Vegas, NV: Kingfisher.

Terban, M., & DeVore, J. (1998). *Scholastic dictionary of idioms.* New York: Scholastic.

Terban, M., & Maestro, G. (1993). *It figures! Fun figures of speech.* New York: Scholastic.

Website Resources

Angel Fire Idiom Games
www.www.angelfire.com/wi3/englishcorner/idioms/idioms.html

Food Idioms and Sayings
www.learnenglish.de/vocabulary/eatingidioms.htm

The Idiom Connection
www.idiomconnection.com

Paint by Idioms
www.funbrain.com/idioms

Quia Face Idioms
www.quia.com/jg/66234.html

Quiz-Tree Idioms
www.quiz-tree.com/American_Idioms_main.html

Idioms

Directions: Look at each idiomatic expression and draw a picture of its literal meaning. Then, find the real definition and write a sentence that uses the expression, like in the example below.

Expression	Pictures
as alike as two peas in a pod	P P P P P P P P P +

Definition: to be very similar; nearly the same

Sample sentence(s): *Juan and his brother are as alike as two peas in a pod.*

Expression #1	Pictures
	+

Definition:

Sample sentence(s):

Expression #2	Pictures
	+

Definition:

Sample sentence(s):

Interactive Word Walls

What Is It?

Interactive word walls (Cunningham & Allington, 1999) are used to help reinforce word patterns and high-frequency words. A main word wall is a large bulletin board where students add about five new words each week. Words are listed in alphabetical order. Other types of word walls may be utilized for subject-area classification, thematic units, special word study (e.g., parts of speech, phonemic awareness, compound words), student names, high-frequency words, chunking words, and so on. For best results, students need to actively interact with the word wall (via routine cheers and chants, frequent reviews, and games and activities).

Why Is It Used?

The strategy is used to (1) allow students to internalize both the spelling and meaning of targeted vocabulary words; (2) provide students with a readily available reference when reviewing vocabulary words and writing; and (3) show students, in the case of thematic word walls, the patterns and relationships among words.

What Do I Do?

1 Create a bulletin board that is divided into areas for different letters of the alphabet.

2 On sentence strips, write new vocabulary words from the text and pin them on the interactive word wall. Introduce the word wall to students and encourage them to utilize the word wall when they are writing.

3 As the interactive word wall will be used as an ongoing resource, encourage the class to add new vocabulary words to the word wall that they encounter in the text. Students may also keep a "file" of their own vocabulary cards for their groups for easier access.

4 As an extension activity, students may illustrate words or write additional information about words on the back of their vocabulary cards (e.g., variations of a word, synonyms, sample sentences). As the word wall is meant to be interactive, it is important that the class reviews the wall frequently during the unit.

5 Refer to the word wall often. The interactive word wall is meant as an additional reference for students to use in their writing and understanding of text. Facilitate daily experiences with the word wall, such as chanting the words, asking students to ask questions to try to guess a word that you are thinking of, allowing students to create sentences with various words, and so on.

How Do I Differentiate It?

What if you don't have a free wall to create an interactive word wall? Joyce Jefferson provides her third-grade groups with poster boards to create their own interactive word walls. Since her students have varying abilities and background experiences, Ms. Jefferson allows students to draw words and use invented spelling to expose themselves to the largest variety of words possible. Other teachers allow students to create their own interactive word walls on their desks. The point of interactive word walls is to provide students with another visual tool to assist them in their expressive vocabulary.

Example

Michele Chung's fifth-grade students were exploring the origins of the U.S. government, from the signing of the Declaration of Independence to the writing of the Constitution. (The unit goals are shown in Figure 8.1.) To begin the unit, she began reading aloud the book *The Signers: The 56 Stories Behind the Declaration of Independence* (Fradin & McCurdy, 2002). As they would be spending 3 weeks covering this time period, Mrs. Chung created a thematic word wall for social studies. She divided the wall into 16 boxes (Allen, 1999) and labeled each box with one to three letters. She listed a number of words on 3" × 5" cards that she knew students would encounter in the text and pinned them in alphabetical order in each box (see Figure 8.2). She introduced the wall and the words to students and asked the class to discuss what they thought each word meant. After she read passages from the text, she again asked students to discuss meanings for words. Mrs. Chung encouraged students to make their own word cards for their small groups. Students drew pictures, listed synonyms, and wrote sample sentences (among other things) to help

GRADE 5 HISTORY/SOCIAL SCIENCE GOALS

After unit lesson, students will be able to:

1. Discuss the meaning of the Declaration of Independence and explain its significance.
2. Explain the significance of the new Constitution of 1787, including the struggles over its ratification and the reasons for the addition of the Bill of Rights.
3. Understand the fundamental principles of American constitutional democracy, including how the government derives its power from the people and the primacy of individual liberty.
4. Understand how the Constitution is designed to secure our liberty by both empowering and limiting central government and compare the powers granted to citizens, Congress, the president, and the Supreme Court with those reserved to the states.

FIGURE 8.1. Goals for Ms. Chung's unit on the origins of the U.S. government.

A	B	C	D
American Revolution Approve authorize	Bill of Rights brave	colony committee Constitution Continental Congress convention convince	Declaration of Independence delegate democracy dissolve divided
E–F election Founding Fathers framework	**G** government governor	**H–I** independence instrumental invade	**J–K** justice
L–M legislature liberty loyal merchant militiamen military	**N–O** noble opponent	**P–Q** patriot Philadelphia plantation political prominent proponent protest punishment	**R–S** ratification rebel representation retreat revolution sacrifice separation signature surrender
T taxation transform	**U–V** unanimous	**W** wartime weapon willingness wounded	**X–Y–Z**

FIGURE 8.2. Example of a thematic word wall on the U.S. Constitution.

them remember the meanings of each new vocabulary word. Mrs. Chung told students that they would review the words each day through chants, games, and other activities.

References

Allen, J. (1999). *Words, words, words: Teaching vocabulary in grades 4–12.* Portland, ME: Stenhouse.

Cunningham, P. M., & Allington, R. L. (1999). *Classrooms that work: They can all read and write* (2nd ed.). New York: Longwood.

Text Resources

Fradin, D., & McCurdy, M. (2002). *The signers: The 56 stories behind the Declaration of Independence.* New York: Scholastic.

Lawson, D. (1979). *The changing face of the Constitution.* Boston: Little, Brown.

Levy, E., & Rosenblum, R. (1987). *If you were there when they signed the Constitution.* New York: Scholastic.

Meltzer, M. (1990). *The Bill of Rights: How we got it and what it means.* New York: HarperCollins.

Morris, R. (1985). *Witnesses at the creation: Hamilton, Madison, Jay and the Constitution.* Boston: Henry Holt.

Spier, P. (1987). *We the people: The Constitution of the United States of America.* New York: Doubleday.

Website Resources

A Roadmap to the U.S. Constitution
library.thinkquest.org/11572

Constitution Facts
www.constitutionfacts.com

U.S. National Archives and Records Administration
www.archives.gov

Word Wall

A	B	C	D
E–F	**G**	**H–I**	**J–K**
L–M	**N–O**	**P–Q**	**R–S**
T	**U–V**	**W**	**X–Y–Z**

WORD PLAY:
Hink Pinks, Hinky Pinkies, and Hinkity Pinkities

Hink pinks are riddles in which the answers are words that rhyme with each other and contain the same amount of syllables. Therefore, hink pinks have single-syllable answers, hinky pinkies have two-syllable answers, and hinkity pinkities have three-syllable answers. Students get a kick out of creating these rhyming riddles, and they are an especially good way for students to acquire new vocabulary words. Some examples include:

"Hink Pinks"

plump feline = fat cat

reptile roast = snake bake

cunning insect = sly fly

coal house = black shack

angry employer = cross boss

artificial dessert = fake cake

headache = brain pain

"Hinky Pinkies"

glass gun = crystal pistol

rose downpour = flower shower

useful sweet = handy candy

whale washer = blubber scrubber

a Norseman on wheels = biking Viking

"Hinkity Pinkities"

the White House = president's residence

frozen mode of transportation = icicle bicycle

messing up a pretty answer = solution pollution

sore coverage = infection protection

loving combination = affection connection

WEBSITE RESOURCE

Wuzzles & Puzzles
www.wuzzlesandpuzzles.com/hinkpinks
This site offers anyone age 10 and up a variety of word and math puzzles, mazes, brain teasers, and more. The site provides hours and hours of printable, thinkable fun, boasting over 1,100 free printable puzzles.

K–W–L Plus

What Is It?

K–W–L plus (Ogle, 1986, 1992) is an instructional strategy used to allow students an active role before, during, and after reading an expository text. It requires students to focus on four questions, the first two before they read and the latter two after they read: What I know (K), What I want to know (W), What I learned (L), and What I still need to learn (+). K–W–L plus focuses on the meanings of words as well as passages and what works best with students reading informational materials.

Why Is It Used?

This strategy is used to (1) engage students' interest by making them active participants in their reading; (2) allow students to brainstorm and categorize their ideas prior to reading informational text; (3) clarify to students the purpose(s) of their reading; and (4) encourage students to constantly ask themselves questions before, during, and after their reading.

What Do I Do?

1 Choose an expository text and select a key topic to be covered in that text.

2 Provide each student with his or her own K–W–L plus strategy sheet.

3 Ask students to brainstorm what they know about the topic ("K"). Record student responses on the chalkboard or on an overhead transparency while students record their responses on their strategy sheets.

4 As students provide ideas, ask them questions such as "Where did you learn that?" and "How might you prove it?"

5 Encourage students to review the completed column of information they know about the topic and try to place the different types of information into categories. If students have initial difficulty identifying categories, suggest a couple of categories by relating what students will be reading to other topics previously covered in class.

6 While students brainstorm different pieces and categories of information they know about the topic, record any areas of interest students want to know about but are uncertain about ("W"). Ask students to record any questions they want answered before they read.

7 Allow students to read the text. For particularly difficult texts, preview the text with students and/or allow them to read the texts in parts.

8 Following students' reading of the text, ask them to write down the answers to their questions ("L"). Discuss answers as a whole class, recording student responses on the chalkboard or on the overhead transparency.

9 Ask students to share questions they had that were not answered by the text or any new questions they developed while reading. Record these questions ("+") and discuss where students may be able to obtain answers to these questions.

How Do I Differentiate It?

Contrary to popular belief, K–W–L plus does not have to be a teacher-led activity for the entire class. Kamal Kya encourages his sixth graders to constantly utilize the K–W–L plus model when they are reading about a new topic. His students have successfully worked together in pairs and small groups. Some prefer to discuss just what they know, want to know, learned, and still want to know, while others insist on writing down their experiences. Again, the format lends itself to students adapting as they feel fit.

Example

Maria Vasquez's third graders were learning about important American landmarks, symbols, and essential documents. (The unit goals are shown in Figure 9.1.) Earlier in the week she had shown her students a book of photographs of various American landmarks and asked them whether they recognized any. Today, she told students that they were going to continue to learn about important American landmarks and

---

GRADE 3 HISTORY-SOCIAL SCIENCE GOALS

After unit lesson, students will be able to:

1. Describe the histories of important American landmarks, symbols, and essential documents (e.g., the U.S. flag, the bald eagle, the Statue of Liberty, the U.S. Constitution, the Declaration of Independence, the U.S. Capitol).
2. Determine how landmarks, symbols, and essential documents create a sense of community among American citizens.
3. Identify historical individuals responsible for and/or associated with various American landmarks, symbols, and essential documents (e.g., Benjamin Franklin, Thomas Jefferson, Betsy Ross, Abraham Lincoln, Clara Barton, Cesar Chavez, Martin Luther King Jr.).
4. Describe how landmarks, symbols, and essential documents exemplify cherished American ideals.

FIGURE 9.1. Goals for Ms. Vasquez's unit on American landmarks, symbols, and documents.

symbols by reading a book about Independence Day, July 4th, and learn about why Americans celebrate this day. She showed her class the book *Fireworks, Picnics and Flags: The Story of the Fourth of July Symbols* (Giblin, 2001) and asked students whether they could identify various symbols on the book's cover (e.g., the American flag, the Statue of Liberty). Ms. Vasquez distributed K–W–L plus strategy sheets to the class and asked students to brainstorm what they knew about Independence Day. Students volunteered different information they knew about the Fourth of July, and then the entire class described ways they could classify their information into categories. Ms. Vasquez asked student volunteers to share some of their information, and she wrote their responses on the chalkboard in the "K" column of her chart (see Figure 9.2). After naming six categories, the class looked at the list of things they knew and placed each piece of information into one of the categories. Ms. Vasquez asked each student to write down questions he or she had about the Fourth of July under the "W" category of his or her chart, and she modeled on the chalkboard a few sample questions that students provided. After students read a selection from the book, Ms. Vasquez asked them to write down the answers to their questions under the "L" column of their strategy sheets. She then asked for student volunteers to share some of the things they learned from their reading, and she wrote their responses on the chalkboard K–W–L plus chart. Finally, Ms. Vasquez asked the class to share some of the new questions they had regarding Independence Day. She listed students' questions on the chalkboard under the "+" column and asked them to write their own questions on their strategy sheets. She asked students where they might find the answers to their questions and told them they would continue studying more about important American landmarks, symbols, and essential documents throughout the week.

K What we know	W What we want to know	L What we learned	+ What we still need to learn
(5) fireworks (2) apple pie (2) hot dogs (2) Liberty Bell (1) Independence Hall (1, 2) Statue of Liberty (3) Declaration of Independence (4) Benjamin Franklin (4) George Washington (4) Thomas Jefferson (1) White House (5) parades (2) American flag (3) National Anthem (6) Fourth of July	Why do we celebrate the Fourth of July? Why is the Fourth of July on the 4th of July? Why is Benjamin Franklin on $100 bills? What is the Declaration of Independence? Why do we have fireworks on the Fourth of July?	Thomas Jefferson wrote the Declaration of Independence. The Declaration of Independence made America independent from the British. The Declaration of Independence was adopted on July 4, 1776, in Philadelphia in Independence Hall. Benjamin Franklin, Thomas Jefferson, and many others signed the Declaration of Independence.	Why is Benjamin Franklin on $100 bills? Why did Benjamin Franklin never become President? How come the first American flag had only 13 stars? Why did we keep fighting the British after we signed the Declaration of Independence? Does any other country have a Declaration of Independence? Why was the Declaration of Independence signed in Philadelphia, and not in Washington, DC?

Categories of information we expect to see:
1. landmark
2. symbol
3. essential document
4. historical figure
5. celebration activity
6. important date

FIGURE 9.2. Example of K–W–L Plus. Ms. Vasquez asked students to categorize the information they knew associated with Independence Day. She numbered the categories that the class provided and wrote the number of the appropriate category to the left of each piece of information that students had listed in the "K" section of the chart. The "K" section represents the key vocabulary words the class would be using as they discussed "Independence Day."

References

Ogle, D. M. (1986). K–W–L: A teaching model that develops active reading of expository text. *The Reading Teacher, 39*, 564–570.

Ogle, D. (1992). KWL in action: Secondary teachers find applications that work. In E. K. Dishner, T. W. Bean, J. E. Readence, & D. W. Moore (Eds.), *Reading in the content areas: Improving classroom instruction* (3rd ed.). Dubuque, IA: Kendall/Hunt.

Text Resources

Anderson, D. (2002). *Arriving at Ellis Island*. New York: World Almanac Education.

Giblin, J. (2001). *Fireworks, picnics and flags: The story of the Fourth of July symbols*. New York: Clarion Books.

Gottlieb, S. (2001). *American icons*. Niwot, CO: Roberts Rinehart.

Sherron, V. (1997). *Cherokee Nation v. Georgia: Native American rights*. New York: Enslow.

Sorensen, L. (1994). *The White House*. New York: Rourke.

Uschan, M. (2003). *The California gold rush*. New York: World Almanac Education.

Website Resources

Ben's Guide to Symbols of Government
bensguide.gpo.gov/3-5/symbols

National Historic Landmarks Program
www.nps.gov/nhl/KIDS.htm

National Park Service: The Great American Landmarks Adventure
nps.gov/history/HPS/PAD/adventure/landmark.htm

K–W–L Plus

K What we know	W What we want to know	L What we learned	+ What we still need to learn

Categories of information we expect to see:

1.
2.
3.
4.
5.
6.
7.
8.
9.
10.

List–Group–Label

What Is It?

List–group–label (Taba, 1967; Tierney, Readence, & Dishner, 1995) is an instructional strategy used to help students see how words can belong in a variety of groups. Originally developed to assist children in dealing with technical vocabulary in science and social studies, this brainstorming technique allows students to systematically improve their vocabulary and categorization skills when dealing with a particular content area.

Why Is It Used?

The strategy is used to (1) encourage students to improve their vocabulary and categorization skills, (2) assist students in remembering and reinforcing new vocabulary, and (3) allow students to organize their verbal concepts.

What Do I Do?

1   As a prereading activity, choose a topic from the text and ask students to brainstorm words related to this topic. Write all student suggestions on a piece of butcher paper on the wall.

2   Tell students to look at the list and try to find words that are related to one another. As a whole class, group these words and determine a category name that can serve as a label for this group of words.

3   Ask students to work with partners and determine ways to classify their words, following the example practiced as a whole class. After students figure out a way to group various words, they should write the words on a piece of paper and create a name for each category of words.

4 Ask students to share their categories as a whole class and discuss why they grouped various words together. Write students' words and categories on a separate sheet of butcher paper.

5 Ask students to read the text and identify any new words they encounter as they read.

6 When students are finished reading, ask them to try to place the new words they read into the categories they established earlier.

How Do I Differentiate It?

Janine Grillo often "wordstorms" with her fourth graders. Wordstorming is simply a variation of list–group–label that she uses with her students to help them find connections between words they are familiar with. Many of her students enjoy the class discussion that ensues during a wordstorm, as students get to explain in their own words (and, more importantly, in language that their peers understand) what different words and expressions mean, where they have learned or been exposed to words previously, and how they can properly use the words. The activity never takes longer than 10 minutes, and Mrs. Grillo credits the activity with increasing her students' interest in acquiring new vocabulary.

Example

LaTonya Hall's first graders were excited about the leaves changing colors. She told the class that the leaves were changing colors because of the change in seasons, and she told them that they would be studying all sorts of things about changes in weather. (The unit goals are shown in Figure 10.1.) She taped a piece of butcher paper to the chalkboard and asked her class whether anyone could think of a word related to weather. She printed notes with a marker as students provided her with a variety of responses. The entire class read the list together, and Mrs. Hall told her students that now they had to try to think of words that had things in common. On a separate sheet of butcher paper, she wrote the terms *cloudy*, *rain*, and *wind*, and asked students what these words had in common. A girl said that they were all ways of saying what the weather was like outside, and Mrs. Hall wrote "types of weather" on another piece of butcher paper. She wrote *cloudy*, *rain*, and *wind* under the catgory and asked students to share more words that described types of weather outside. She told students to work together in partners and determine which words were related. Afterward, the class shared their words and categories (see Figure 10.2). Mrs. Hall told the class to pay attention to the words when she read aloud the book *On the Same Day in March: A Tour of the World's Weather* (Singer, 2000) and look for any new words that they had not discussed earlier. As she read the book, she stuck pieces of tape next to words that students told her sounded like

---

GRADE 1 SCIENCE GOALS

After unit lesson, students will be able to:

1. Understand how to use simple tools (e.g., thermometer, wind vane) to measure weather conditions and record changes from day to day and across the seasons.
2. Recognize that the weather changes from day to day, but that trends in temperature or of rain (or snow) tend to be predictable during a season.
3. Explain that the sun warms the land, air, and water.

FIGURE 10.1. Goals for Mrs. Hall's unit on weather.

Initial Brainstorm (List)

Weather Words		
storm	hurricane	icy
cloudy	thunder	jacket
rain	lightning	thermometer
wind	blizzard	desert
sunny	traffic	mountains
temperature	tank top	shorts
cold	sweater	flood
hot	summer vacation	seasons
tornado	weatherman	accidents

Categorization (Group–Label)

Weather Words	
1. types of weather	cloudy, rain, wind, sunny, thunder, lightning
2. storms	tornado, hurricane, flood, cloudy, rain, wind, thunder, lightning, blizzard
3. temperature	hot, cold, temperature
4. types of clothes	tank top, sweater, jacket, shorts
5. things that happen because of weather	traffic, accidents, summer vacation, seasons
6. places with different weather	desert, mountains
7. ways to know about weather	temperature, thermometer, weatherman

FIGURE 10.2. Example of list–group–label.

weather words. Once she finished the book, she slowly reread the book aloud to the class and added the words with tape to their class list of weather words. Finally, the whole class discussed where to classify the new words.

References

Taba, H. (1967). *Teacher's handbook for elementary social studies*. Reading, MA: Addison-Wesley.

Tierney, R. J., Readence, J. E., & Dishner, E. K. (1995). *Reading strategies and practices: A compendium* (4th ed.). Boston: Allyn & Bacon.

Text Resources

Branley, F. M. (2000). *Snow is falling*. New York: HarperCollins.

dePaola, T. (1985). *The cloud book*. New York: Holiday House.

Gibbons, G. (1990). *Weather words and what they mean*. New York: Holiday House.

Hesse, K. (1999). *Come on, rain!* New York: Scholastic.

Singer, M. (2000). *On the same day in March: A tour of the world's weather*. New York: HarperCollins.

Wiesner, D. (1992). *Hurricane*. Boston: Houghton Mifflin.

Website Resources

Fun with Words
www.fun-with-words.com

Kids Web—Weather
Eo.ucar.edu/webweather

The Weather Dude
www.wxdude.com

List–Group–Label

Initial Brainstorm (List)

Categorization (Group–Label)

WORD PLAY:
Tom Swiftlies

I hate "dull" vocabulary words. Journalists are taught to use dull words constantly (e.g., they must consistently use the expression *said*, instead of varying it with terms like *exclaim*, *pronounce*, and so on). To prevent the overuse of dull words, I used to hand students paint strips (you can get paint strips from any paint store, and paint strips usually feature colors that advance from dull to rich) and ask them to write a dull word in the dull color (e.g., *pretty*) and write richer words for each progressive box (e.g., *pretty* becomes *beautiful*, which becomes *gorgeous*, which becomes *stunning*). Tom Swiftlies are another way to direct students' attention to dull language.

Tom Swiftlies (also known as "Tom Swifties") are phrases in which a quoted sentence is linked by a pun to the manner in which it is attributed (e.g., "We must hurry," said Tom swiftly). The name is a ridicule of the writing style found in the *Tom Swift* series of books in which the author, Victor Applegate, went to great trouble to avoid repetition of the unadorned word *said*. Many famous writers such as Stephen King despise the use of adverbs, preferring to focus on using stronger verbs instead. Tom Swiftlies are a good way to introduce puns to students and point out the importance of using "stronger" vocabulary words. Some examples for students include:

"Do you think I'm a dull person?" Tom asked bluntly.

"I might as well be dead," Tom croaked.

"Pass me the shellfish," said Tom crabbily.

"Would you like to ride in my new ambulance?" asked Tom hospitably.

"We just struck oil!" Tom gushed.

"Lights, camera, action!" Tom said directly.

WEBSITE RESOURCES

Jokes N Jokes Tom Swifties
www.jokesnjokes.net/funny.jokes.amusing.humor.laughs/General/swifties001.htm
Good starting point for those interested in Tom Swifties.

Tom Swifties
tomswifty.com
Provides numerous examples.

Morphemic Analysis

What Is It?

Morphemic analysis (Manzo & Manzo, 1990; O'Rourke, 1974) is an instructional strategy used to help students determine a word's meaning through examination of its prefix, root, and/or suffix. It is recommended to use as an "incidental" approach in which teachers watch for words in reading assignments that may be unfamiliar to students but have familiar word parts.

Why Is It Used?

The strategy is used to (1) assist students in generating the meaning of new words they encounter based on their knowledge of morphemes (prefixes, suffixes, roots); (2) introduce common spelling and meaning patterns based on word parts; and (3) demonstrate to students that, with the knowledge of a small number of morphemes, students can decipher the meanings of many new vocabulary words.

What Do I Do?

1 Read aloud a passage to students and ask them to tell you when you read a word they do not understand.

2 Using a chalkboard or an overhead projector, list each new vocabulary word.

3 After reading the passage, select one of the new vocabulary words from the list. Divide the word into its morphological components and identify the meaning of each component.

4 Write the word in the context of a sentence from the text. Discuss the meaning of the word in the sentence.

5 Again, look at the word's separate morphemes and discuss how they create the meaning of the word.

6 Distribute morphemic analysis chart (MAC) handouts (see Figure 11.2 below) that list prefixes, roots, and suffixes, along with their meanings. Present a new vocabulary word to students and ask them to underline the word's morphemes, using their handouts as guides.

7 Ask students to work in pairs. Tell partners to copy the list of new words, underline each word's morphemes (using their MAC as a guide), and use the underlined morphemes to determine the meaning of each word. When students think they have an answer, ask them to explain their reasoning to one another.

8 When students conclude this exercise, ask them to share the morphemes and meanings of words they found. If they correctly predict a word's meaning, write it under the word on the chalkboard or on an overhead transparency.

9 As an extension, encourage the class to create an MAC for a bulletin board that keeps track of the various morphemes they know. As students learn new morphemes, they may add their definitions and examples to the chart.

How Do I Differentiate It?

Rey Gonzalez believes in teaching his kindergartners prefixes and suffixes, as he argues that nearly 90% of words with prefixes contain one of 20 prefixes, and only 10 suffixes comprise nearly 90% of words with suffixes. How does he teach young students prefixes and suffixes? In his approach to morphemic analysis, Mr. Gonzalez encourages his students to create their own words with prefixes and suffixes. For example, while *un-* is the most commonly used prefix, the first one he teaches his kindergartners is *anti-*. In that way, he finds boys raising their hands saying they are "anti-homework" and "anti-time out." Then he teaches the students *pro-*, and sees a barrage of hands raised by students claiming to be "pro-recess" and "pro-pizza party." While Mr. Gonzalez does not encourage other teachers to focus solely on the smallest parts of words, he has found this differentiated approach is a fun way to encourage students to see how words are constructed and to use that knowledge to deconstruct other words' meanings.

Example

Amir Zarawani told his sixth graders that many words, especially in math, are formed by combining "morphemes," which he explained were the smallest units of language that convey meaning. He said that, as a part of their math lessons, they would begin to learn the Greek and Latin "morphemes" (root words, prefixes, and suffixes) that are used to construct many of the words they use in English. (The unit goals are shown in Figure 11.1.) By understanding morphemes, he told his students, they would be able to figure out what many new words meant. Mr. Zarawani discussed some examples of prefixes, root words, and suffixes and explained their meanings to the class. He told them he was going to read aloud a passage from a fun math book called *The Number Devil: A Mathematical Adventure* (Enzensberger & Berner, 2000) and asked students to clap whenever he read a word that they did not understand or had one of the morphemes that they had discussed. After reading the passage, he listed the words on the chalkboard. Next, he highlighted the first word from his list, *circumference*, and divided it into three parts (*circum + fer + ence*). He defined what each morpheme meant and asked the class to guess the meaning of the word. When they correctly predicted what the word meant, he wrote their definition under the word. He distributed MACs (see Figure 11.2) to the class and asked them to work in pairs. Using the information on the charts, students needed to copy the math terms from the chalkboard and underline each word's morphemes, define the word, write the word in the "example" section of their MAC, and explain to each other how they determined the word's meaning. After 15 minutes, Mr. Zarawani asked students to share their responses as a whole class. He told students that they would create a bulletin board that listed various morphemes and encouraged them to play with morphemes and create their own words.

GRADE 6 MATH GOALS

After unit lesson, students will be able to:

1. Analyze problems by identifying relationships, distinguishing relevant from irrelevant information, identifying missing information, sequencing and prioritizing information, and observing patterns.
2. Formulate and justify mathematical conjectures based on a general description of the mathematical question or problem posed.
3. Determine when and how to break a problem into simpler parts.

FIGURE 11.1. Goals for Mr. Zarawani's unit on morphemes in math.

Math Words of the Day: decimal, perimeter, circumference, diameter, geometry, polygon, triangle, process, base, diagram

1. *circumference*—circum- (around) + fer (bear, carry) + -ence (thing) = circumference (carry around thing)
2. *decimal*—decim- (ten) + -al (pertaining to) = decimal (pertaining to ten)
3. *perimeter*—peri- (around, near) + meter (measure) = perimeter (measure around)
4. *diameter*—dia- (through, across) + meter (measure) = diameter (measure across)
5. *geometry*—geo- (earth) + metr (measure) + -y (activity) = geometry (measure earth activity)
6. *polygon*—poly- (many) + -gon (angle) = polygon (many angles)
7. *triangle*—tri- (three) + angl (angle) + -e (pertaining to, thing) = triangle (three-angle thing)
8. *process*—pro- (forward) + -cess (going) = process (forward going)
9. *base*—bas- (low) + -e (pertaining to, thing) = base (low thing)
10. *diagram*—dia- (through, across) + gram (something written, mass) = diagram (something written across)

Morphemic Analysis Chart (MAC)

PREFIXES		
Prefix	**Meaning**	**Examples**
decim-	ten	*decimal*
peri-	around, near	*perimeter*
circum-	around	*circumference*
dia-	through, across	*diameter*
geo-	earth	*geometry*
poly-	many	*polygon*
tri-	three	*triangle*
pro-	forward	*process*
bas-	low	*base*
ex-	out	*external*
centi-	hundred	*centimeter*
milli-	thousand	*milliliter*
circl-	circle	*circle*
angl-	angle	*angle*
plan-	flat	*plane*
com-, con-, col-, co-	with, together	*combine, construct, collect, coordinate*
dis-	not, opposite from	*disconnect*
pre-	before	*predict*

ROOTS		
Root	**Meaning**	**Examples**
meter/metr	measure	*perimeter, diameter, geometry*
fer	bear, carry	*circumference*
angl	angle	*triangle*
gram	something written, mass	*diagram, milligram*
ology	study of	*biology*
chrono	time	*chronology*
dict	say	*predict*
hemi	half	*hemisphere*
struct	build	*construct*
par	equal	*compare*

(cont.)

FIGURE 11.2. Example of morphemic analysis. Students are responsible for filling in examples of words that use the appropriate prefix, root, or suffix.

SUFFIXES		
Suffix	**Meaning**	**Examples**
-al	pertaining to	*decimal*
-ence	thing	*circumference*
-y	activity	*geometry*
-gon	angle	*polygon*
-e	pertaining to, thing	*triangle, base*
-cess	going	*process*
-sect	cut, divide	*intersect*
-ble	likely to be	*probable*

FIGURE 11.2. *(cont.)*

References

Manzo, A., & Manzo, U. (1990). *Content area reading: A heuristic approach.* Upper Saddle River, NJ: Merrill/Prentice Hall.

O'Rourke, J. P. (1974). *Toward a science of vocabulary development.* Hague, The Netherlands: Morton.

Text Resources

Anno, M. (1987). *Anno's math games.* New York: Philomel.

Du Bois, W. P. (1986). *The twenty-one balloons.* New York: Puffin Books.

Enzensberger, H. M., & Berner, R. S. (2000). *The number devil: A mathematical adventure.* New York: Henry Holt.

Pappas, T. (1997). *The adventures of Penrose the mathematical cat: The mathematical cat.* San Carlos, CA: Wide World/Tetra.

Sachar, L. (1994). *More sideways arithmetic from wayside school.* New York: Scholastic.

Wyatt, V., & Cupples, P. (2000). *The math book for girls and other beings who count.* Toronto, Canada: Kids Can Press.

Website Resources

Dr. Goodword's Vocabulary Games
   www.alphadictionary.com/ww/goodwordjr

Mathematical Morphemes
   www.duboislc.net/math/FractionWords.html

Math Words
   www.pballew.net/etyindex.html

Word Roots and Prefixes
   www.virtualsalt.com/roots.htm

Morphemic Analysis Chart (MAC)

PREFIXES		
Prefix	**Meaning**	**Examples**

ROOTS		
Root	**Meaning**	**Examples**

SUFFIXES		
Suffix	**Meaning**	**Examples**

Personal Vocabulary Journals

What Is It?

Personal vocabulary journals (Graves & Slater, 1996; Searfoss, Readence, & Mallette, 2001) are journals used by students for recording new vocabulary words and concepts that they are learning. Vocabulary journals can take a variety of formats and may include dictionary definitions, personal definitions and reflections, examples of words used in context of readings, student drawings, graphs, charts, and so on.

Why Is It Used?

The strategy is used to (1) improve the scope and accuracy of word choice in students' writing, (2) encourage students to explore reference tools such as journals and dictionaries as tools to use for independent vocabulary growth, (3) provide students with a format for adding new words to their vocabulary knowledge and actively processing these words, and (4) encourage students to chart their vocabulary growth.

What Do I Do?

1 Make personal vocabulary journals with students for each curricular area. One easy approach is to have students staple 10 to 15 sheets of lined paper between two pieces of construction paper that will serve as the personal vocabulary journal's cover. Ask students to write their names and the title of the curricular area (e.g., "mathematics vocabulary journal") on their personal vocabulary journal covers.

2 Personal vocabulary journals are used as an ongoing activity. To that end, model various types of vocabulary journal activities that students can perform before, during, and after their reading. Some examples of activities include taking notes, drawing diagrams, listing new vocabulary words, writing personal reflections, and using illustrations to remember key concepts.

3 Encourage students to work carefully and neatly. Although personal vocabulary journals are meant as additional tools for students to use in acquiring vocabulary, they may also be used in students' growth portfolios to demonstrate their progress.

4 Assign specific personal vocabulary journal activities and model expectations. For example, if students are studying fractions, show them how to turn math problems into word problems and vice versa. Encourage students to be creative with their personal vocabulary journals.

5 Ask students to turn in their personal vocabulary journals and review their notes and questions. Provide feedback where necessary.

How Do I Differentiate It?

Personal vocabulary journals, perhaps more than any other strategy, take on the unique characteristics of each student, as students themselves decide how to store vocabulary words for future reference. Some students may use pictures and photographs to remember target vocabulary words, while others may use words in sentences and list formal definitions. The nice thing about personal vocabulary journals is that they may be used for a variety of different subjects and themes, and students can experiment with a variety of different entry formats.

Example

Nwanke Ogbu's second graders love funny poems that rhyme, so Mr. Ogbu checked out a number of funny poetry books from the public library (because he is a teacher, his local public library allows him to check out 50 books at a time). He read the bilingual book of poems *Gathering the Sun: An Alphabet in Spanish and English* (Flor Ada & Silva, 2000) to the class. (The unit goals are shown in Figure 12.1.) Many of his students understood the poems in Spanish and English. Mr. Ogbu told his students to get out their personal vocabulary journals for language arts so that they could add new words that they learned from the poems. All of his students had their own photocopied handouts of the book, and Mr. Ogbu said that he would read the book again very slowly while students followed along on their handouts. He asked students to use a yellow crayon and highlight any new words that they heard as he read. After he finished reading, he asked his students to copy all of the words they highlighted and select five to seven words to write in their personal vocabulary journals (see Figure 12.2). He told students they could write more words if they had extra time, but he wanted them to concentrate on the five to seven words that they thought would be most important for them to learn. After students wrote their words, Mr. Ogbu told them to copy the sentences that contained the words and asked them to try to guess the definitions of the words. Finally, he told his students to write down ways that could help them remember the words (e.g., sentences, pic-

---

GRADE 2 LANGUAGE ARTS GOALS

After unit lesson, students will be able to:

1. Memorize a poem.
2. Recite poetry individually and together chorally.
3. Read a poem and determine what it is about.
4. Recognize the rhyming words from a selection.
5. Identify the use of rhythm, rhyme, and alliteration in poetry.

FIGURE 12.1. Goals for Mr. Ogbu's unit on poetry.

Language Arts Journal for ___Viridiana___

Gathering the Sun: An Alphabet in Spanish and English by Alma Flor Ada

Vocabulary word	My definition	How and where the word was used in my reading	Ways to help me remember what the word means (sentences, pictures, etc.)	
sprout	pop up; grow	"yet your example and your words sprout anew in the field rows . . ." from "César Chávez"		
drowsy	sleepy	"Are the flowers drowsy stars that lie sleeping in the fields?" from "Stars or Flowers"	I get drowsy late at night. My grandfather is drowsy when he takes me to school because he just gets out of bed when we leave.	
honor	caring about things	"Honor is the work we do in the fields. Honor is a family who loves and cares for one another" from "Honor"	My grandfather does nice things for people because he has honor. People who tell the truth have honor. People who lie don't.	
wrinkled	lots of lines; old	"Small, curly, fresh and wrinkled heads of bright green lettuce" from "Lettuce"	My grandfather has wrinkled skin. My shirt got wrinkled in the laundry.	
tucked	put away tightly	"In the field row lies a seed, all tucked in like a baby in a crib" from "Field Row"	My grandfather tucks me into bed. My favorite book is tucked away in the library corner.	

FIGURE 12.2. Example of student's personal vocabulary journal.

tures). He encouraged students to take their personal vocabulary journals home to get more examples of how to use the words from their parents and caregivers.

References

Graves, M. F., & Slater, W. H. (1996). Vocabulary instruction in the content areas. In D. Lapp, J. Flood, & N. Farnan (Eds.), *Content area reading and learning: Instructional strategies* (2nd ed., pp. 261–275). Boston: Allyn & Bacon.

Searfoss, L. W., Readence, J. E., & Mallette, M. H. (2001). *Helping children learn to read: Creating a classroom literacy environment* (4th ed.). Boston: Allyn & Bacon.

Text Resources

Bagert, B., & Arnold, T. (2002). *Giant children.* New York: Dial Books for Young Readers.

Brown, C. (1999). *Polkabats and octopus slacks: 14 stories.* Boston: Houghton Mifflin.

Flor Ada, A., & Silva, S. (2000). *Gathering the sun: An alphabet in Spanish and English.* New York: Scholastic.

Florian, D. (1998). *Insectlopedia.* Orlando, FL: Harcourt.

Greenberg, D. T. (1999). *What ever happened to Humpty Dumpty?* Boston: Little, Brown.

Lansky, B., & Carpenter, S. (1997). *No more homework no more tests.* New York: Meadowbrook.

Prelutsky, J., & Stevenson, J. (1990). *It's raining pigs and noodles.* New York: Greenwillow.

Website Resources

Fern's Poetry Club
pbskids.org/arthur/games/poetry

Funny Poetry for Children
gigglepoetry.com

Instant Poetry Forms
Ettcweb.LR.K12.NJ.us/forms/newpoem.htm

Poetry for Kids Links
poetry4kids.com/

Wizards & Pigs
learninggamesforkids.com/word_games/word_games_wizardpigs.html

Personal Vocabulary Journal

Journal for _____

Vocabulary word	My definition	How and where the word was used in my reading	Ways to help me remember what the word means (sentences, pictures, etc.)

WORD PLAY:
Dittograms

Dittograms (Wegryn, 2004) are words and phrases with repeated sounds (e.g., the nose knows, mite might). Challenge students to try their hands at putting homophones together. The trick is to see how many dittograms you can get into one coherent sentence. Here are some examples:

Although she can't cant, she certainly can can-can.

Eight ate late last night.

Coarse courses can cause cavities.

Can you smell the foul fowl?

Adam Lambert is an idle idol.

Hoarse horses horse around.

The score is two to two (three homophones in a row).

TEXT RESOURCES

Wegryn, J. (2004). *A barrel full of words.* New York: iUniverse.
Wegryn, J. (2007). *Words to tickle the humorous humerus.* New York: iUniverse.

WEBSITE RESOURCE

A Barrel Full of Words
www.jimwegryn.com/Words/Homophones.htm

Jim Wegryn, author of the fabulous book *Words to Tickle the Humorous Humerus* (2007), showcases a collection of over 2,500 English words and phrases in humorous context on this site, including "goofinitions," mock antonyms, and much more. Tons of excellent vocabulary games that actively engage learners of all ages.

Possible Sentences

What Is It?

Possible sentences (Moore & Moore, 1986, 1992; Moore, Readence, & Rickelman, 1989) is an instructional strategy that uses some of the vocabulary words students will encounter in a text in order to heighten their curiosity. Using this strategy, students use their broad knowledge of a subject to predict how words might be used in a given text and write sentences that might possibly be found in the text.

Why Is It Used?

The strategy is used to (1) arouse students' interest in the text to be read by allowing them to make predictions about the text's contents; (2) help students make predictions on their own about the meanings and relationships of unfamiliar words in texts to be read; and (3) encourage students to present their ideas to one another, justify their ideas, listen to others' points of view, and evaluate their own definitions.

What Do I Do?

1 Write key vocabulary terms from the text on the chalkboard or on an overhead transparency. Pronounce each word, and make sure that each word can be defined by using the text.

2 Ask students to select pairs of words from the list. For each pair, have students write a sentence that they think might appear in the text.

3 Ask student volunteers to write their sentences on the chalkboard, underlining the words the students have included from the list.

4 Discuss sentences. Ask whether anyone disagrees with any of the sentences.

5 Have students read the text on their own to verify the accuracy of their sentences.

6 Discuss sentences again as a class. Have students evaluate sentences for accuracy, and ask them to make any changes they wish.

7 Ask students to create additional sentences based on information from the text.

8 Encourage students to record their sentences in their notebooks for further study.

How Do I Differentiate It?

Possible sentences is typically used as a writing activity, but a number of teachers offer the strategy to students in a variety of ways. The sixth-grade teachers at Alameda Academy decided in their professional learning community to differentiate possible sentences by allowing students to work with partners orally (e.g., recording their sentences on cassette tapes, creating improvisational skits that use the target vocabulary words, videotaping possible sentences "newscasts"). Because many of their students are learning English as a second language, the activity also promotes speaking and listening skills.

Example

Kate Schwartz's fifth graders enjoyed the math games she used to teach them how to reason. (The unit goals are shown in Figure 13.1.) Mrs. Schwartz believed that the best way to get students interested in math was to make math fun and relate it to their everyday lives. Often, she found, her students would get "hung up" on problems because they did not understand some of the terms. Today, she listed a number of terms that students would be reading about in a math text she had photocopied for them. Mrs. Schwartz asked students to select partners, and she gave each team one or two words. She asked all student teams to write down sentences that used the vocabulary words (see Figure 13.2). Volunteers wrote sentences on the chalkboard for the whole class to discuss. Next, students read the copies of the text. After hearing the words in the story, some students asked whether they could change the sentences they had created because they had used their words incorrectly. Again, Mrs. Schwartz asked volunteers to write their sentences on the chalkboard for the rest of the class to discuss. Mrs. Schwartz concluded the lesson by asking students to add additional sentences in their journals that illustrated the meanings of their vocabulary words. She asked students to have their partners check their work to make sure that their sentences made sense.

GRADE 5 MATHEMATICS GOALS

After unit lesson, students will be able to:

1. Analyze problems by identifying relationships, distinguishing relevant from irrelevant information, sequencing and prioritizing information, and observing patterns.
2. Determine when and how to break a problem into simpler parts.
3. Use estimation to verify the reasonableness of calculated results.
4. Apply strategies and results from simpler problems to more complex problems.
5. Evaluate the reasonableness of the solution in the context of the original situation.
6. Develop generalizations of the results obtained and apply them in other circumstances.

FIGURE 13.1. Goals for Mrs. Schwartz's unit on understanding math terms.

Terms	
probability	error
mode	conclusion
median	data
mean	case
statistics	estimate
frequency	generate
chance	conditional
proportion	likelihood

Mrs. Schwartz hands Vijay and Deondre the words *frequency* and *generate*. The partners write the following sentences:

1. The *frequency* of wins for our professional basketball team is high.
2. The team *generates* a lot more ticket sales when they win.

Vijay and Deondre read the text and decide their sentences are fine. Mrs. Schwartz asks them to write a few more sentences to make sure that there is no doubt they understand.

1. The *frequency* of wins for our professional basketball team is high. They make their shots with high *frequency*. The rest of the NBA is tired of the *frequency* that our team wins championships.
2. The team *generates* a lot more ticket sales when they win. That is because our team *generates* a lot more points. If other teams would *generate* more points, they might beat our team.

FIGURE 13.2. Example of possible sentences developed by students.

References

Moore, D. W., & Moore, S. A. (1986). Possible sentences. In E. K. Dishner, T. W. Bean, J. E. Readence, & D. W. Moore (Eds.), *Reading in the content areas: Improving classroom instruction* (pp. 179–183). Dubuque, IA: Kendall/Hunt.

Moore, D. W., & Moore, S. A. (1992). Possible sentences: An update. In E. K. Dishner, T. W. Bean, J. E. Readence, & D. W. Moore (Eds.), *Reading in the content areas: Improving classroom instruction* (pp. 179–183). Dubuque, IA: Kendall/Hunt.

Moore, D. W., Readence, J. E., & Rickelman, R. J. (1989). *Prereading activities for content area reading and learning* (2nd ed.). Newark, DE: International Reading Association.

Text Resources

Markle, S. (1993). *Math mini mysteries.* New York: Scott Foresman.

Pittman, H. (1996). *A grain of rice.* New York: Skylark.

Scieszka, J. (1995). *Math curse.* New York: Viking.

Tahan, M. (1993). *The man who counted: A collection of mathematical adventures.* New York: W. W. Norton.

Tang, G. (2001). *The grapes of math: Mind-stretching math riddles.* New York: Scholastic.

Wick, W. (1998). *Walter Wick's optical tricks.* New York: Cartwheel Books.

Website Resources

Aplus Math
www.aplusmath.com

Cool Math
www.coolmath.com

Cool Math 4 Kids
www.coolmath4kids.com

Fun Brain Math
www.funbrain.com

Math Is Fun
www.mathisfun.com/games/index.html

Word Problems for Kids
www.mystfx.ca/special/mathproblems

Possible Sentences

```
┌─────────────────────────────────────┐
│              Terms                   │
│                                      │
│                                      │
│                                      │
│                                      │
│                                      │
│                                      │
│                                      │
│                                      │
│                                      │
│                                      │
│                                      │
└─────────────────────────────────────┘
```

For each word, write a sentence that uses that word. Can you determine what the word means by reading your sentence?

_____

_____

_____

_____

_____

_____

Read the text. Was your word used the same way as the text used it? Write more sentences that use your word.

_____

_____

_____

_____

_____

_____

_____

_____

Read-Alouds

What Is It?

Read-alouds (Brassell, 2006; Krashen, 2005; Trelease, 2006) are one of the simplest, most enjoyable, and most effective strategies for enhancing students' vocabulary knowledge. By reading a variety of texts (fiction and nonfiction), teachers can engage students in text by modeling and asking and answering questions.

Why Is It Used?

The strategy is used to (1) allow students to actively listen and interpret information from text, (2) introduce new words and concepts by building on students' prior knowledge through reader and listener interactions, and (3) sensitize students to different patterns in different texts (e.g., fiction/nonfiction, magazines, letters).

What Do I Do?

1 Choose a text. Remember that different read-alouds require different formats (e.g., reading a magazine article to students is different than reading a chapter book, and reading about the human digestive system is different than reading about child prodigies). Keep in mind that since you are reading the text, you may choose texts that are above your students' level.

2 Before you begin to read the text, announce the name of the book, author, and illustrator, and remind students to ask questions if they do not understand something. If you are continuing a book, ask students to review what has happened so far in the text.

3 Establish a warm climate for read-alouds. Allow students to get comfortable, whether they are lying on a carpet in front of you or sitting at their desks throughout the classroom. If students want to draw or doodle as you read, let them, as long as they pay attention to the story.

4 On a poster board or piece of butcher paper, create a vocabulary chart of new terms that you encounter in the text. As an extension activity, students may create illustrations to help them remember each term, or they can write sample sentences.

5 If the book has pictures, ask students to describe what is happening in the pictures. Whether a book has pictures or not, you can check for students' understanding by occasionally asking them what is going on in the book and why particular events occur. Another way to keep students involved is to ask them what they think is going to happen next, how the text is similar to their own experiences, and what they would do under similar circumstances.

6 As you read, use plenty of expression (e.g., gestures, pacing, intonation).

7 After you read, allow plenty of time for discussion. Allow students to ask questions and make comments about the book.

8 Provide students with time to read on their own and make sure that they have plenty of interesting materials to choose from (if you are leading a unit on nutrition, it would be a good idea to have a lot of books related to that topic available). It is vital that you read while students read.

How Do I Differentiate It?

There are countless ways to differentiate read-alouds. Teachers can treat different text types in different ways (e.g., reading aloud a newspaper article should sound different than reading aloud a love letter or reading aloud a narrative). Teachers can vary their voices, dress up, read in different places in the classroom, set different moods (e.g., light a candle and turn off the lights, play different types of music in the background, allow students to lie down). Dina Palmer reads aloud stories for all ages to her 11th-grade chemistry class. It only takes 10 minutes of class time, and she finds that it focuses her students on the rest of her class (she always chooses science-oriented books or articles to read aloud). As a way to integrate technology with her reading program, Siobhan Raj encourages her second graders to go to the Book-Pals Storyline website (listed in website resources), which features various celebrities reading aloud award-winning books. By discussing target vocabulary words before and after readings, both teachers agree that read-alouds offer a fun, nonintimidating way for students to develop their vocabulary knowledge.

Example

Phonna Nguyen read aloud to her fifth graders at least three times a day. She found it to be her most effective classroom management plan, and students told her they enjoyed all of the stories that she read to them. She usually selected three types of books (easy, familiar, and difficult) and would read them at different points in the day. As her class had become fascinated with books she had been reading to them about how the human body functions, Ms. Nguyen tried to find all sorts of entertaining books that explained human biology in an understandable way. (The unit goals are shown in Figure 14.1.) As most of the books she had were fairly long, she chose to read books in short chunks or by chapters. For example, after lunch each day she would read a chapter from *Fantastic Voyage* (Asimov, 1976). One of Ms. Nguyen's students told her that his brother was reading *Fantastic Voyage* in his eighth-grade class, and that motivated Ms. Nguyen's students to want to read it for themselves. During science time, Ms. Nguyen began reading segments from *Grossology* (Branzei & Keely, 2002). She began by asking students to talk about the various bodily functions they had read about. As students discussed various functions, body parts, and ailments, Ms. Nguyen wrote new vocabulary words on a piece of butcher paper and suggested that students could create their own picture dictionaries of biological facts if they continued to work so hard (see Figure 14.2). Students excitedly reacted as one boy talked about drawing pictures of snot. After everyone laughed, Ms. Nguyen read aloud a passage from the text that dealt with diarrhea. She asked students questions and tried to answer some of theirs. When she could not answer a student's question, Ms. Nguyen suggested students consult parents or other adults, try to find the answer on the Internet, or consult a librarian. It took nearly 25 minutes for Ms. Nguyen to get through the passage, but all students were engaged. After they finished the passage, Ms. Nguyen taught the entire class the book's diarrhea song, and students worked in groups to try to create picture dictionaries for all of the various health terms they had learned to that point.

GRADE 5 SCIENCE/HEALTH GOALS

After unit lesson, students will be able to:

1. Understand that many multicellular organisms have specialized structures to support the transport of materials.
2. Explain the sequential steps of digestion and the roles of teeth and the mouth, esophagus, stomach, small intestine, large intestine, and colon in the function of the digestive system.
3. Understand the role of the kidney in removing cellular waste from blood and converting it into urine, which is stored in the bladder.
4. Describe how animal cells break down sugar to obtain energy, resulting in water (respiration).

FIGURE 14.1. Goals for Ms. Nguyen's unit on human body functions.

Read-Aloud Vocabulary		
Book title: *Grossology* by S. Branzei & J. Keely		
Context	**Word(s)**	**Meaning**
"Barf: here comes dinner! Your mouth begins to water; your stomach muscles clamp; you take a deep breath as you race toward the bathroom; you stand above the porcelain master; your throat and mouth open. Rrrrraaaaalllllllffffff. Dinner is revisiting.	barf, upchucking, puked, throwing up clamp porcelain master revisiting	vomit tighten toilet coming back; returning
After a really heavy bout of upchucking, some people say they puked their guts out. This claim just isn't true. Your guts stay right where they are; only the stuff in the gut's holding tank is expelled. If you conducted a barf analysis for the contents of puke before flushing or cleaning it up, you would find out a lot about throwing up."	bout conducted analysis flushing	attack tried; started study wash out

FIGURE 14.2. Example of a vocabulary chart created by students from a read-aloud.

References

Brassell, D. (2006). *Readers for life: The ultimate reading fitness guide* (grades K–8). Portsmouth, NH: Heinemann.

Krashen, S. (2005). *The power of reading* (2nd ed.). Portsmouth, NH: Heinemann.

Trelease, J. (2006). *The read-aloud handbook* (6th ed.). New York: Penguin Books.

Text Resources

Arnold, N., & DeSaulles, T. (1999). *Disgusting digestion*. New York: Scholastic.

Asimov, I. (1976). *Fantastic voyage*. New York: Bantam Books.

Branzei, S., & Keely, J. (2002). *Grossology*. New York: Price Stern Sloan.

Parker, S. (1999). *How the body works*. New York: Reader's Digest Adult.

Pringle, L. P. (2000). *Taste*. New York: Benchmark Books.

Solheim, J. (1998). *It's disgusting and we ate it! True food facts from around the world and throughout history*. New York: Simon & Schuster.

Swanson, D., & Cowles, R. (2001). *Burp! The most interesting book you'll ever read about eating*. New York: Kids Can Press.

Website Resources

BookPals Storyline Online
www.storylineonline.net

The Human Body
kids/connect.com/subject-index/31-health/337-human-body.html

PBS Kids Between the Lions Read Alouds
pbskids.org/lions/stories

Read Alouds: Trelease On Reading
www.trelease-on-reading.com/

Your Digestive System
kidshealth.org/kid/htbw/digestive_system.html

WORD PLAY:
Book Talk

Every week you should lead a "book talk" with your students. Whenever I lead a book talk, I include books for all ages, as adults need to read more children's books and children need to be read aloud more adult-level books. We know that the best way to improve our vocabularies is to read a lot, and this book talk focuses on reading materials that have a particular focus on words. (If you'd like to hear all about these books, make sure to attend one of my vocabulary presentations, where I pitch each book with the zeal of a carnival barker!)

TEXT RESOURCES

Children's Books

Cleary, B. P. (2001). *Hairy, scary, ordinary: What is an adjective* (Words Are Categorical Series). Minneapolis, MN: Carolrhoda Books.

Fine, E. H. (2004). *Cryptomania: Teleporting into Greek and Latin with cryptokids.* New York: Tricycle Press.

Gwynne, F. (2005). *A chocolate moose for dinner* (Stories to Go Series). New York: Aladdin.

O'Connor, J. (2005). *Fancy Nancy.* New York: HarperCollins.

Parrish, P. (2005). *Amelia Bedelia* (series). New York: Greenwillow.

Scieszka, J. (2005). *Baloney* (*Henry P.*). New York: Puffin.

Terban, M. (2007). *Eight ate: A feast of homonym riddles.* London: Sandpiper.

Young Adult Books

Aurandt, P. (1984). *Paul Harvey's the rest of the story.* New York: Bantam.

Clement, A. (1998). *Frindle.* New York: Aladdin.

Snicket, L. (1999). *A bad beginning* (A Series of Unfortunate Events Series). New York: HarperCollins.

White, E. B. (2001). *Charlotte's web.* New York: HarperCollins.

Adult Books

Allen, J. (1999). *Words, words, words: Teaching vocabulary in grades 4–12.* Portland, ME: Stenhouse.

Fry, E. B. (2004). *The vocabulary teacher's book of lists.* San Francisco: Jossey-Bass.

Harrington Elster, C. (2005). *What in the word? Wordplay, word lore, and answers to your peskiest questions about language.* New York: Harvest Books.

Winchester, S. (2005). *The professor and the madman: A tale of murder, insanity, and the making of the Oxford English dictionary.* New York: Harper Perennial.

WEBSITE RESOURCE

The Lazy Readers' Book Club
www.lazyreaders.com

I created the Lazy Readers' Book Club as I learned from speaking across the country that many people use "lack of time" as their primary excuse for not reading. As we know that reading is the best way to build vocabulary, this site includes monthly recommendations of books for children, young adults, and adults. Each book is under 250 pages. In addition, the site offers free vocabulary games for students to download.

Scavenger Hunts

What Is It?

Scavenger hunts (Cunningham, Moore, Cunningham, & Moore, 1995; Vaughn, Crawley, & Mountain, 1979) can be used as an instructional strategy to enhance students' vocabulary through the gathering of objects and pictures to represent concepts that need to be developed more fully for students.

Why Is It Used?

The strategy is used to (1) allow students to sharpen their reference skills and become involved and interested in the topic to be studied, (2) provide students with direct and indirect experience with unfamiliar words through the collection of objects and pictures, and (3) help students develop word meanings as they relate to topics (since objects and pictures being sought all relate to the same topic).

What Do I Do?

1 From a text, create a list of unfamiliar vocabulary words that deal with the concept to be studied (e.g., for a unit on measurement: pounds, miles, degrees, minutes).

2 Take all of the words from the list that can be represented by pictures and objects and add some familiar words that can be represented by pictures or objects until you have a list of approximately 10 represented objects that relate to the topic (e.g., measuring tape, clock, scale). You now have your final scavenger hunt list.

3 Have students form small groups of three to four and give each group a scavenger hunt list. If possible, give student groups their scavenger hunt lists a week or two before the unit is to be taught.

4 Tell groups that they have 1 to 2 weeks to find as many objects and pictures with the words from the list as they can.

5 Provide students with time to search for the words in class as well as out of class. Encourage students to use library books, encyclopedias, magazines, textbooks, newspapers, dictionaries, Internet resources, junk mail, environmental print, and any other resources to find the words on the list.

6 Encourage students to collect different types of objects and pictures and assign points for each object they bring (e.g., 4 points for building a model or collage representing the word, 3 points for bringing a picture of the word, 2 points for finding a book about the word, 1 point for drawing the word or using the word in a sample sentence).

7 Allow class time for groups to meet to discuss the words and strategize how they plan to find objects and pictures for each word. Remind groups that they are competing with other groups so they should try to keep their progress secret.

8 On the day when all scavenger hunt items are due, ask groups to organize all of their objects and pictures by each word they represent. Allow groups to assign points to other groups' work. The group with the most points can be responsible for creating a bulletin board for the unit, featuring the objects and pictures they provided.

How Do I Differentiate It?

More and more teachers across the country seem to be using scavenger hunts as a web-based activity, as scavenger hunts lend themselves perfectly to addressing state and federal technology standards while maintaining the interest of students. Jezebel Campos encourages her students to find target vocabulary words on a number of different sites in a number of different contexts. (Warning: while scavenger hunts are safe on most school district computers because of sophisticated blocking devices, these activities are not recommended on home computers unless teachers communicate closely with parents about the dangers of Internet browsers that permit all online content.) Victor Pacheco incorporates safe web-based scavenger hunts when he creates WebQuests (see website resources below).

Example

Cindy Rodriguez read her class the book *Millions to Measure* (Schwartz & Kellogg, 2003) and told her third graders that they would be studying a unit on weights and measures in a couple of weeks. (The unit goals are shown in Figure 15.1.) She selected 10 words from *Millions to Measure* and other books she would be reading to her students about different forms of measurement, and she photocopied lists

---

GRADE 3 MATHEMATICS GOALS

After unit lesson, students will be able to:

1. Use appropriate math vocabulary.
2. Use concepts of probability such as likely, unlikely, and certain.
3. Estimate and explain measurements of length and weight.
4. Measure and understand length, weight, temperature, area, and time using standard and nonstandard units of measurement.

FIGURE 15.1. Goals for Mrs. Rodriguez's unit on weights and measures.

of the words for students. Mrs. Rodriguez gave the lists to all of her students and asked them to form small groups. Mrs. Rodriguez told the groups that they would be playing a game known as a "scavenger hunt." She explained that each group needed to try to collect as many pictures and objects as possible that illustrated each word from their measurement vocabulary list (see Figure 15.2.). She told students that she would give them class time to try to find photos in books and magazines or to draw pictures and write sentences with the words, but she told them that the team that looked for objects and pictures outside of school would probably find the most items. She promised students that the group that found the most items from the scavenger hunt list would get to decorate an entire bulletin board with all of their objects. Throughout the week Mrs. Rodriguez allowed students about 30 minutes a day to research the words with their teams, and students also used any extra time they had when they finished their other work early. The following week, students brought all of their objects and pictures to class, and Mrs. Rodriguez asked the class to decide which group had found the most pictures and objects that illustrated their scavenger hunt words. The group that won spent time after school the rest of the week decorating their bulletin board with all of the "measurement memorabilia" that they had collected.

ruler	gallon
thermometer	weight
scale	centimeter
minutes	temperature
degrees	miles

FIGURE 15.2. Example of a scavenger hunt list.

References

Cunningham, P. M., Moore, S. A., Cunningham, J. W., & Moore, D. W. (1995). *Reading and writing in elementary classrooms: Strategies and observations*. New York: Longman.

Vaughn, S., Crawley, S., & Mountain, L. A. (1979). A multiple-modality approach to word study: Vocabulary scavenger hunts. *The Reading Teacher, 32,* 434–437.

Text Resources

King, A. (1998). *Measuring weight and time: Math for fun.* Brookfield, CT: Copper Beech Books.

Lasky, K., & Hawkes, K. (1994). *The librarian who measured the Earth.* Boston: Little, Brown.

Lewis, J. P., & Remkiewicz, F. (2002). *Arithme-tickle: An even number of odd riddle-rhymes.* New York: Silver Whistle.

Myller, R. (1962). *How big is a foot?* New York: Atheneum.

Pallotta, J., & Bolster, R. (2003). *Apple fractions.* New York: Cartwheel Books.

Schwartz, D. M., & Kellogg, S. (2003). *Millions to measure.* New York: HarperCollins.

Website Resources

AAA Math—Third Grade
   www.aaamath.com/B/grade3.htm

Interactive Units Converter
   www.convert-me.com/en

Taking America's Measure
   www.nist.gov/public_affairs/kids/kidsmain.htm

Webquest.Org
   webquest.org

Semantic Feature Analysis

What Is It?

Semantic feature analysis (Nagy, 1988; Pittleman, Heimlich, Berglund, & French, 1991; Ruddell, 2001) is an instructional strategy used to help develop vocabulary by understanding relationships between words. It is often used as a prereading activity in which students identify important similarities and differences among a group of concepts. Students may create a grid to help them visualize connections, make predictions, and master important concepts. By analyzing the semantic features of words, students can develop word associations and extend their content knowledge by eliciting their prior knowledge.

Why Is It Used?

The strategy is used to (1) visually represent key words or concepts, (2) introduce new words or concepts by building on prior knowledge, (3) distinguish relationships among words or concepts being taught, and (4) strengthen conceptual understanding of information.

What Do I Do?

1 Select a key word or concept and ask students to give examples.

2 Create a grid. In the left-hand column, list key vocabulary words or phrases related to the topic category.

3 In a row across the top of the grid, ask students to suggest some attributes or characteristics (semantic features) shared by key vocabulary words or phrases.

4 Model with students an analysis of each key vocabulary word or phrase in terms of each feature. Use a plus sign (+) to indicate that the feature applies to the vocabulary word, and use a minus sign (-) to indicate that the feature does not. If it is not obvious whether a feature applies, put a question mark in the square and encourage students to discuss.

5 Brainstorm with students for additional words or phrases that may be added to the row.

6 Practice marking whether features apply to different words or phrases. If students mark the same pattern of pluses and minuses for more than one word, challenge them to identify features that will differentiate between these terms. The more practice they have with grids, the more proficient and independent students will become.

7 Brainstorm with students for additional features that may be added.

8 Encourage students to explain the rationale behind their markings.

9 Work with students to complete the grid with plus and minus signs.

10 Discover and discuss with students the uniqueness of each word. Encourage students to add words and features to the grid as they acquire more information during and after reading.

How Do I Differentiate It?

Semantic feature analysis works as a great way to promote vocabulary and comprehension in students. Although many teachers use it as a whole-group activity, plenty of other teachers allow students to complete a semantic feature analysis in small groups, with a partner or individually. Amy Rabun allows her third graders to choose whether they'd like to work on their semantic feature analysis grids individually, in pairs, or in small groups (some years, the majority of students select partners, while other years her students prefer to work in small groups). She then permits students to present their findings however they want. One of the most popular ways her students present their grids is through puppet shows (students get behind a cardboard box and use hand puppets to present their grids to the class). In this way, semantic feature analysis has become an extremely popular vocabulary activity in Ms. Rabun's third-grade class from year to year.

Example

Tamekia Johnson's fourth-grade class was studying different American geographic regions and the similarities and differences between regions. (The unit goals are

---

GRADE 4 HISTORY/SOCIAL SCIENCE GOALS

After unit lesson, students will be able to:

1. Identify different geographic regions of the United States.
2. Describe how different geographic regions vary in vegetation, wildlife, and climate.
3. Explain differences in land use, population density, architecture, services, and transportation according to geographic region.

FIGURE 16.1. Goals for Mrs. Johnson's unit on U.S. geographical regions.

shown in Figure 16.1.) Mrs. Johnson created a semantic feature analysis grid on the chalkboard and explained that students would select regions of the United States for the left-hand column (see Figure 16.2). The class then brainstormed features that regions shared or did not share. While the list was not exhaustive, Mrs. Johnson reminded students that they could add features and regions to the grid at any time. The class brainstormed features that distinguished regions and discussed their rationale. In some cases, the class could not agree. For example, some students believed that many mountains had ski resort developments while others pointed out that most mountains were remote. Mrs. Johnson did not tell students whether they were "right" or "wrong" but rather encouraged students to read more about various regions in order to further support their point of view.

Concept: Geographic Regions of the United States

	heavily populated	soil used for farming	developed	hot	wildlife	boats used for transport	tornadoes	little water
valleys/prairies	+	+	+	+	+	−	+	?
mountains	−	−	?	−	+	−	−	−
coastline (beaches)	+	−	+	?	+	+	−	−
deserts	−	−	−	+	+	−	−	+
forests	−	+	−	−	+	+	−	−
swamps/wetlands	−	−	−	?	+	+	−	−

+ = Students believe feature is true of that region.

− = Students believe region lacks that feature.

? = Students disagree whether region matches feature; students will seek answer in their reading.

FIGURE 16.2. Example of a semantic feature analysis grid.

References

Nagy, W. (1988). *Teaching vocabulary to improve reading comprehension.* Newark, DE: International Reading Association.

Pittleman, S., Heimlich, J., Berglund, R., & French, M. (1991). *Semantic feature analysis.* Newark, DE: International Reading Association.

Ruddell, R. (2001). *Teaching children to read and write: Becoming an effective literacy teacher* (3rd Ed.). Boston: Allyn & Bacon.

Text Resources

Bial, R. (1996). *Mist over the mountains: Appalachia and its people.* New York: Houghton Mifflin.

George, J. G., & Brenner, F. (1996). *One day in the desert.* New York: HarperCollins.

Hobbs, W. (1999). *Maze.* New York: HarperCollins.

National Geographic Society. (2001). *National geographic guide to the national parks of the United States.* Washington, DC: National Geographic Society.

Schmidt, T., Schmidt, J., & Mumford, W. (2001). *Saga of Lewis & Clark: Into the uncharted west.* New York: DK Publishing.

Staub, F. (1994). *America's wetlands.* New York: Lerner Publishing Group.

Website Resources

Just Curious: Environmental Science
   www.suffolk.lib.ny.us/youth/jcsenvironment.html

National Geographic Expeditions
   nationalgeographicexpositions.com

United States Geography Games
   www.gamequarium.com/usgeography.html

U.S.A. Games
   www.sheppardsoftware.com/web_games.htm

Semantic Feature Analysis

Category: _____   **Name:** _____

Examples

WORD PLAY:
Pangrams

A pangram is a sentence that contains all letters of the alphabet. Interesting pangrams are generally short ones; constructing a sentence that includes the fewest repeat letters possible is a challenging task. However, pangrams that are slightly longer yet enlightening, humorous, or eccentric are noteworthy in their own right. Pangrams are a great way to entice students to "play with language." Some examples of pangrams (with the number of total letters used in each sentence) include:

The quick brown fox jumps over the lazy dog. (35 letters)

The five boxing wizards jump quickly. (31 letters)

Crazy Fredericka bought many very exquisite opal jewels. (48 letters)

Jaded zombies acted quaintly but kept driving their oxen forward. (55 letters)

Six big juicy steaks sizzled in a pan as five workmen left the quarry. (56 letters)

WEBSITE RESOURCE

RinkWorks
rinkworks.com/words/pangrams.shtml

RinkWorks is a privately owned entertainment website based in New Hampshire, committed to offering site users productions that range from the serious to the silly. The site includes numerous fun word games.

Semantic Mapping

What Is It?

Semantic mapping (Blachowicz & Johnson, 1994; Heimlich & Pittleman, 1986; Pittleman, Heimlich, Berglund, & French, 1991), also known as "semantic webbing," is an instructional strategy used to clarify and enrich students' understandings of new vocabulary words. It uses a graphic organizer resembling a spider web to organize information by categories. Semantic mapping is a variation of semantic feature analysis that allows students to visually represent the relationships between concepts and words.

Why Is It Used?

The strategy is used to (1) visually represent key words or concepts, (2) introduce new words or concepts by building on prior knowledge, (3) distinguish relationships among words or concepts being taught, and (4) strengthen conceptual understanding of information.

What Do I Do?

1 Select a key word or concept and enclose the word in a box in the center of the chalkboard or on an overhead transparency.

2 Ask students to form small groups and brainstorm words related to the key word or concept.

3 List students' suggested words on the chalkboard or overhead and group into broad categories.

4 Ask students to name categories and suggest additional ones.

5 Discuss the semantic map as a class. For further clarification, connect categories with lines to the key word or concept. Relationship words may be written on the lines.

How Do I Differentiate It?

Semantic mapping lends itself to differentiation because it allows students to graphically display background knowledge of different target vocabulary words. Getting to that point, however, can take different forms in the roles various students play. While some students may prefer writing down what they know about new target vocabulary words and concepts, others may be better at orally describing what they know. Other students may prefer presenting their findings to the class as a whole. By placing students with various strengths in different small groups, the teacher can allow them to confidently participate and contribute in this vocabulary-building exercise.

Example

Rogelio Martinez's second graders were beginning a unit on dinosaurs. (The unit goals are shown in Figure 17.1.) He wanted his students to understand how scientists could prove dinosaurs' existence and why the dinosaurs became extinct. Mr. Martinez wrote the word *dinosaurs* on the chalkboard and asked students to organize into groups of three to four. Next, he asked the groups to brainstorm among themselves all of the words that they could think of associated with dinosaurs. He told the groups to pay attention to characteristics words shared so that they could categorize them under subheadings. After about 5 minutes, Mr. Martinez asked the groups to dictate the words they came up with, and he wrote them on the chalkboard. He encouraged students to place words under categories. For example, when students shared the words *ancient* and *old*, Mr. Martinez explained that dinosaur remains were also known as "fossils" and placed the terms under that category. Later, when students said that dinosaurs had lived on *land* and in *water*, a student suggested that Mr. Martinez categorize those terms under "Earth." After further discussion, students asked Mr. Martinez to connect categories with the key word *dinosaur* by writing relationship words on the connecting lines. For example, one student asked Mr. Martinez to connect *dinosaurs* with *food* with the word *ate*. Finally, Mr. Martinez told students to add words and categories to the semantic map as they learned more about dinosaurs (see Figure 17.2).

GRADE 2 SCIENCE GOALS

After unit lesson, students will be able to:

1. Say that fossils provide evidence about the plants and animals that lived long ago on Earth.
2. List characteristics of dinosaurs.
3. Describe conditions that may cause a species to become extinct.
4. Explain how scientists learn about the past history of the earth by studying fossils.

FIGURE 17.1. Goals for Mr. Martinez's unit on dinosaurs.

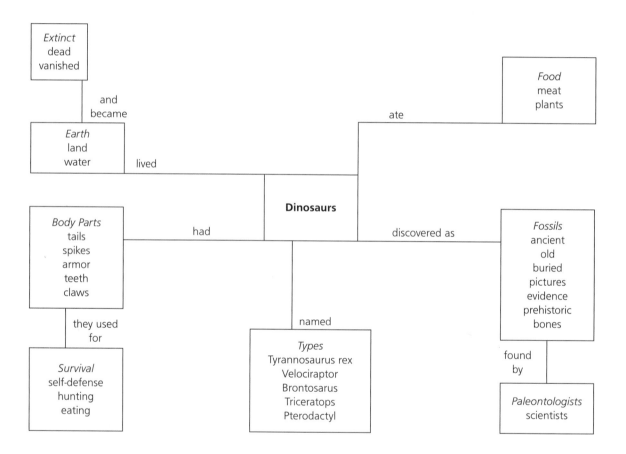

FIGURE 17.2. Example of a semantic map on dinosaurs.

References

Blachowicz, C. L. Z., & Johnson, B. E. (1994). Semantic mapping. In A. Purves (Ed.), *Encyclopedia of English studies language arts* (pp. 116–127). New York: Scholastic.

Heimlich, J. E., & Pittleman, S. D. (1986). *Semantic mapping: Classroom applications.* Newark, DE: International Reading Association.

Pittleman, S., Heimlich, J., Berglund, R., & French, M. (1991). *Semantic feature analysis.* Newark, DE: International Reading Association.

Text Resources

Aliki. (1998). *Digging up dinosaurs.* New York: HarperTrophy.

Barton, B. (1990). *Bones, bones, dinosaur bones.* New York: Ty Crowell.

Brighton, C. (1999). *The fossil girl: Mary Anning's dinosaur discovery.* Brookfield, CT: Millbrook Press.

Cole, J. (1995). *The magic school bus in the time of the dinosaurs.* New York: Scholastic.

Pringle, L. P. (1996). *Dinosaurs: Strange & wonderful.* New York: Penguin.

Wahl, J. (2000). *The field mouse and the dinosaur named Sue.* New York: Cartwheel Books.

Website Resources

Dino Base
   dinobase.gly.bris.ac.uk/

Dino Hunt
   www.sjgames.com/dinohunt

Dinosauria
   www.dinosauria.com

Free Graphic Organizers
   www.eduplace.com/graphicorganizer

Mindjet
   www.mindjet.com

Semantic Map

Student VOC Strategy

What Is It?

The *student VOC strategy* (Billmeyer & Barton, 1998; Marzano, Pickering, & Pollock, 2001) is an instructional strategy used to engage students' "whole" brain by tying definitions of new words to the senses. Through this process and discussion, the goal is that students will gain insight and understanding about the specific words they encounter in various texts and continue to develop their skills of learning new words, especially the uses of prediction and reflection in their process of word acquisition.

Why Is It Used?

The strategy is used to (1) help students analyze word meanings from context, (2) allow students to make meaningful sensory connections that relate to their particular learning styles, and (3) enhance students' retention by adding a sensory connection between the reading content and students' prior knowledge.

What Do I Do?

1 List key vocabulary words from the text on the chalkboard or on an overhead transparency.

2 Ask students to identify any word that is new to them or unclear.

3 Tell students that they will be trying to deduce the meanings of the words using the student VOC strategy. Write the following reminder list on the chalkboard or transparency: locate and predict, consult and experiment, and connect and explain. Distribute handouts to students that guide them through the steps of the student VOC strategy.

4 As a class, review the procedures for the student VOC strategy by practicing with one of the key words.

5 Tell students to *locate* the key word in the text and copy the sentence as it appears. On the basis of how the word is used in the text, ask students to *predict* what the word means.

6 Ask students to *consult* a dictionary or friend for the "actual" definition of the key word. Then, tell students to *experiment* using the word by writing it in a sentence.

7 Allow students to *connect* the word with a picture, movement, or past experience they can visualize. Tell students to *explain* their connection device to a partner.

8 Read the text, paying careful attention to key words from the list. Tell students to work in partners and repeat the student VOC strategy for each word.

9 At the conclusion of this exercise, ask students to share their definitions and how they arrived at those definitions.

How Do I Differentiate It?

The student VOC strategy is what differentiated instruction is all about, as it ties in all the senses and learning modalities. Put simply, the student VOC strategy offers something for everybody. When students come across target and new vocabulary words that they do not understand, they are encouraged to determine words' meanings by connecting definitions with what they already know. They can demonstrate prior experiences by creating games, singing songs, making skits, writing stories, and discussing meanings—the student VOC strategy offers a variety of possibilities for teachers to differentiate instructional products.

Example

Victor Nuñez wanted his fifth-grade class of predominantly ELLs to try to find a systematic way of figuring out the meanings of new terms that they encountered in math. (The unit goals are shown in Figure 18.1.) He told the class that they would practice using the student VOC strategy to help determine meanings of new words in the book *The Dot and the Line: A Romance in Lower Mathematics* (Juster, 2001). After reading a certain section of the text out loud (while the students followed along in their own books) containing some of the special vocabulary, Mr. Nuñez asked the students to identify words that were unfamiliar to them. On an overhead

---

GRADE 5 MATHEMATICS GOALS

After unit lesson, students will be able to:

1. Identify angles as vertical, adjacent, complementary, or supplementary and provide descriptions of these terms.
2. Use the properties of complementary and supplementary angles and the sum of the angles of a triangle to solve problems involving an unknown angle.
3. Draw quadrilaterals and triangles from given information about them (e.g., a quadrilateral having equal sides but no right angles, a right isosceles triangle).

FIGURE 18.1. Goals for Mr. Nuñez's unit on geometry.

transparency, he wrote a list of the gathered words. The class then decided on a key word on the list to explore: *parallelogram.* After reading a sentence from the book that had the word, the class decided that the sentence did not help very much when trying to determine the word's definition. Mr. Nunez told the class that many times words are still not clear after reading a sentence. One student suggested looking at the picture in the book, and Mr. Nuñez said that was a good strategy. The teacher told the class, however, that most of the books they would be reading did not have pictures, so the next step in the student VOC strategy was to consult a dictionary or consult with a friend about the definition. The dictionary definition was not very helpful either, because it listed a more difficult word in the definition, so Mr. Nuñez gave some examples. Satisfied that students understood him, Mr. Nuñez asked students to write sentences on their own and show them to their partners. He asked a volunteer to share her sentence, and he wrote the sample sentence on the overhead. Then he asked students to connect the definition by drawing a picture, acting out a motion, or relating the definition to something they had encountered. Some students drew pictures, some made gestures with their hands, and others pointed out objects in the room that could be parallelograms. Mr. Nuñez asked students to explain their ways of remembering parallelograms, then asked them to read the story on their own. Students worked with partners and determined the meanings of the key vocabulary words using the same process. Afterward, the entire class reviewed the definitions they determined for key words (see Figure 18.2).

References

Billmeyer, R., & Barton, M. L. (1998). *Teaching reading in the content areas: If not me, then who?* (2nd ed.). Aurora, CO: Mid-Continent Regional Educational Laboratory.

Marzano, R., Pickering, D., & Pollock, J. (2001). *Classroom instruction that works: Research-based strategies for increasing student achievement.* Alexandria, VA: Association for Supervision and Curriculum Development.

```
┌─────────────────────────────────────┐
│          Vocabulary word             │
│                                      │
│          parallelogram               │
└─────────────────────────────────────┘
```

1. Write the sentence in which the word appears in the text.

For months he practiced in secret. Soon he was making squares and triangles . . . and parallelograms.

2. Based upon how it is used in the text, predict what the word means.

The sentence does not help much. There are pictures, but they show lots of different shapes. It is difficult to understand the word by just looking at this sentence.

3. Consult an "expert" for the actual definition (friend, teacher, dictionary).

The dictionary says a parallelogram is "a quadrilateral whose opposite sides are parallel and equal." That doesn't help much because we don't know what "quadrilateral" means. Mr. Nuñez says a quadrilateral has four sides, but all the sides do not have to be the same (like a square).

4. Show your understanding of the word by using it in a sentence of your own.

The tables that our groups sit at are parallelograms. They look like rectangles, not squares.

5. Choose one of the following ways to help you remember the word's meaning: Draw a picture of what the word means to you, select and perform a miming action that the word reminds you of, or connect the word with something similar that you have heard—a story, a news report, a song. Write down the association or connection you have made.

6. Explain why you chose this way to represent what the word means to you.

Parallelograms have four sides. The sides that are opposite to one another always have to be the same. Rectangles are parallelograms. So are squares. A rhombus is also a parallelogram.

FIGURE 18.2. Example of a student VOC strategy.

Text Resources

Adler, D. A., & Tobin, N. (1998). *Shape up! Fun with triangles and other polygons.* New York: Holiday House.

Field, R. (1990). *Geometric patterns from Roman mosaics: And how to draw them.* New York: Tarquin.

Juster, N. (2001). *The dot and the line: A romance in lower mathematics.* Dallas, TX: Seastar.

Neuschwander, C., & Geehan, W. (2001). *Sir Cumference and the great knight of angleland: A math adventure.* Waterton, MA: Charlesbridge.

Sharman, L. (1994). *The amazing book of shapes: Explore math through shapes and patterns.* New York: DK Publishing.

Stein, S. K. (2001). *How the other half thinks.* Waldoboro, ME: McGraw-Hill.

Website Resources

Cool Math 4 Kids
www.coolmath4kids.com/geometrystuff.html

Line Symmetry
www.adrianbruce.com/Symmetry

The Math Forum, K–12 Geometry
mathforum.org/geometry/k12.geometry.html

Student VOC Strategy

┌───┐
│ **Vocabulary word**   │
│   │
│   │
│   │
└───┘

1. Write the sentence in which the word appears in the text.

2. Based upon how it is used in the text, predict what the word means.

3. Consult an "expert" for the actual definition (friend, teacher, dictionary).

4. Show your understanding of the word by using it in a sentence of your own.

5. Choose one of the following ways to help you remember the word's meaning: Draw a picture of what the word means to you, select and perform a miming action that the word reminds you of, or connect the word with something similar that you have heard—a story, a news report, a song. Write down the association or connection you have made.

6. Explain why you chose this way to represent what the word means to you.

WORD PLAY:
Oxymorons

An oxymoron is a combination of contradictory words. It is a literary figure of speech in which opposite or contradictory words, terms, phrases, or ideas are combined to create a rhetorical effect by paradoxical means. Ask students to search for everyday oxymorons they may hear or see. Here are some examples:

- Almost ready
- Home school
- Jumbo shrimp
- Least favorite
- Long shorts
- Major general
- Mercy killing
- Natural additives
- Recorded live
- Silent alarm

WEBSITE RESOURCES

Ethan's Oxymoron Page
www.ethanwiner.com/oxymoron.html
Includes extensive lists of oxymorons.

Oxymoron List
www.oxymoronlist.com
Huge database of oxymorons.

Thinks.com
thinks.com/words/oxymorons.htm
Showcases a number of "ridiculous word pairings."

Text Talk

What Is It?

Text talk (Beck, McKeown, & Kucan, 2002; Graves & Slater, 1996) is an instructional strategy that is similar to dialogic reading that emphasizes the importance of the talk surrounding text and the active involvement of students during teacher read-alouds. The teacher asks students open-ended questions when reading the text and gradually turns over increased responsibility to students.

Why Is It Used?

The strategy is used to (1) encourage students to respond to open-ended questions by the teacher during read-alouds, using support from language in the text; (2) show students how to use context clues to help determine the meanings of new words; and (3) allow students to interpret story elements based on language found in the text.

What Do I Do?

1 Show students the front cover of a book and tell them that you would like them to listen to the story very carefully because you will not be showing them all of the pictures.

2 Ask students what they think about the front cover and what types of predictions they believe they can make about the story based on the cover.

3 As you read the text, ask students open-ended questions (e.g., describe what is happening in the pictures, recall what happened in the story, relate something from the book to their lives). Another way to get students to participate is to leave words out of a sentence and let students guess what the next word is.

4 As you read the text, ask students whether there are any new words in the text that they do not understand. Write all new words on index cards and place them in a pocket chart where everyone can see them.

5 After finishing the story, read the list of new words to students and then reread the sentence where each word appears in the story.

6 Ask students what clues the story gives about the meaning of the new words.

7 Ask students to give examples of other situations where they might use the new words.

How Do I Differentiate It?

Text talk lends itself to a natural dialogue between readers and their audiences. Different students may look for different meanings in texts, and text talk helps facilitate students' understandings of target vocabulary words. Michele Harvath turns over her text talk to her fifth graders gradually throughout the school year, so that an observer may see Mrs. Harvath guiding the text talk at the beginning of the year but may see the students running a text talk by the end of the year. She often dresses in silly costumes as she reads aloud stories to her class, and her fifth graders follow suit once responsibility for leading a text talk is handed to them. The important thing that Mrs. Harvath has observed over the past 10 years she has been working on text talk with her fifth graders, she says, is that her students never grasp strategies until she introduces them and practices the routines multiple times as a class. Once students understand the basics, she says, they can then create their own variations. She likens text talk to painters, in that good painters learn the basics first and copy their mentors before experimenting with their own styles. Text talk can be differentiated, but according to Mrs. Harvath it is a lot easier to differentiate a text talk once students grasp the standard format.

Example

Harriett King's second graders love it when she reads aloud stories to them. One of their favorite activities is "text talk," when Mrs. King asks students lots of questions as she reads to them. (The unit goals are shown in Figure 19.1.) Today she read the big book *Caps for Sale* (Slobodkina, 1968) to the class. Mrs. King first showed the students the cover of the book and asked them whether they had any ideas about what the story would be about. Students pointed to the man with the moustache lying on a tree branch above a stack of caps and giggled at the sight of a couple of monkeys peeking from behind the tree. They guessed that the story would be about some monkeys stealing the man's caps. As Mrs. King read the story to the students, she asked them a number of questions about what was happening in the story, what

---

GRADE 2 LANGUAGE ARTS GOALS

After unit lesson, students will be able to:

1. Describe story elements (e.g., characters, setting) and recount experiences in a logical sequence.
2. Use knowledge of the author's purpose(s) to comprehend text.
3. Ask clarifying questions about essential textual elements (e.g., why, what if, how).
4. Restate facts and details in the text to clarify and organize ideas.
5. Recognize cause-and-effect relationships in a text.

FIGURE 19.1. Goals for Mrs. King's unit on story texts.

they thought was going to happen next, and what the students would do if they found themselves in a similar situation (see Figure 19.2). When students asked her what a word meant, she wrote the word on an index card and put the word in a pocket chart next to her. After she finished the story, she read all the new words that students had pointed out as she read. She reread the story and had students put sticky notes under all new words as they appeared in the story. When they came across a new word, Mrs. King asked the students whether they could determine what the word meant based on the rest of the sentence. When she finished rereading the story, Mrs. King asked students to make up their own sentences with the new words and tell them to a friend. Finally, students shared some of their sentences they had thought of with the new words.

TEXT TALK
New vocabulary words:

peddler	disturb
ordinary	refreshed
checked	stamped
country	

Sample questions:
1. Looking at the cover, what do you think this book is about?
2. Why does the man have so many caps on his head?
3. Why does the man keep walking up and down the street?
4. What types of different caps does the man have?
5. What do you think happened to the man's caps? Why?
6. What would you do if a bunch of monkeys stole your caps?
7. Have you ever lost something important to you? What did you do?
8. Why was the man so angry? How can you tell he was angry?
9. Why did the monkeys throw the caps back to the ground?

FIGURE 19.2. Example of text talk questions.

References

Beck, I. L., McKeown, M. G., & Kucan, L. (2002). *Bringing words to life: Robust vocabulary instruction.* New York: Guilford Press.

Graves, M. F., & Slater, W., H. (1996). Vocabulary instruction in the content areas. In D. Lapp, J. Flood, & N. Farnan (Eds.), *Content area reading and learning: Instructional strategies* (2nd ed. pp. 261–275). Boston: Allyn & Bacon.

Text Resources

Allard, H., & Marshall, J. (1977). *Miss Nelson is missing!* Boston: Houghton Mifflin.

Andersen, H. C., & Pinkney, J. (1999). *The ugly duckling.* New York: William Morrow.

Brown, M. (1986). *Stone soup.* New York: Simon & Schuster.

Clement, R. (1998). *Grandpa's teeth.* New York: HarperCollins.

Slobodkina, E. (1968). *Caps for sale.* New York: HarperCollins.

Ward, H. (1999). *The hare and the tortoise: A fable from Aesop.* Brookfield, CT: Millbrook Press.

Website Resources

Book Adventure Kids Zone
www.bookadventure.org/ki/index.asp

BookPals Storyline
www.storylineonline.net

Jim Trelease's Read-Aloud Handbook, etc.
www.trelease-on-reading.com

Online Children's Stories
people.ucalgary.ca/~dkbrown/stories.html

PBS Kids Between the Lions—Stories
pbskids.org/lions/stories

Vocabulary Self-Collection Strategy

What Is It?

Vocabulary self-collection strategy (Haggard, 1986; Readence, Bean, & Baldwin, 2001; Ruddell, 1992), also known as vocabulary self-selection (VSS), is an instructional strategy that places the responsibility for learning words on the students. It is a group activity in which students each bring one or two words to the attention of the group that they believe the group should learn. VSS differs from contextual redefinition in that students, rather than the teacher, generate the majority of words to be explored and learned. Students use their own interest and prior knowledge to enhance vocabulary growth.

Why Is It Used?

The strategy is used to (1) help students generate vocabulary words to be explored and learned by focusing on words that are important to them, (2) simulate word learning that occurs naturally in students' lives, and (3) guide students in becoming independent word learners by capitalizing on their own experiences.

What Do I Do?

1 Organize students into small groups of three to five.

2 Ask students to reread or review a text and identify one word that they believe should be studied. Each group should nominate a word. The teacher should choose a word, as well. For younger students, the teacher can reread the text and ask student groups to pay careful attention to words they would like to choose.

3 Provide students with no more than 5 minutes to select a word, determine its definition from the text, and provide a rationale for learning the word.

4 Ask a student representative from each group to nominate a word, describe where the group found the word, explain what the group believes the word means, and tell why the group chose the word.

5 Write words on the chalkboard or on an overhead transparency one word at a time.

6 Discuss each word as a whole class. Expand on each word's meaning by adding whatever personal knowledge or experience students have with the word.

7 Focus on the definition of each word in context and compare and contrast that definition with meanings given from students' prior personal experiences.

8 After the discussion is completed, finalize the word list by eliminating duplicate words, words that students already know, and/or words that students do not want to learn.

9 Hand out VSS sheets (see Figure 20.2 below) to students so that they may individually record the final list of words with their definitions.

10 Use the final vocabulary list to facilitate follow-up activities like word sorts, crosswords, and so on.

How Do I Differentiate It?

Freedom of choice among students is the key to the VSS. By allowing students to select the words that they are interested in learning more about, teachers are empowering their students and encouraging them to take an active interest in their own learning. Frederica Pimmel cautions that some students may require some extra guidance in terms of what types of words they need to focus on. By modeling to students which words in a story are critically important to comprehending the story, teachers can interest students in discovering "the important words to know," according to Mrs. Pimmel. She says that she uses the VSS as a game in which she challenges her third graders to act like "word investigators" who have to uncover the most important words in any passage. By calling the activity a game, she has learned, students take an immediate interest and practice the activity outside of school, as well.

Example

Joyce Tan had been working with her first graders on a thematic unit emphasizing the importance and responsibility of good citizenship. (The unit goals are shown in Figure 20.1.) Her students had been reading a number of stories about how to respect themselves and others, play fairly, and behave like model citizens. Today, the class had read the book *Dear Mrs. LaRue: Letters From Obedience School* (Teague, 2002), and afterward, Ms. Tan asked her students to arrange themselves in groups of four. She told students that she would read aloud the story more slowly and asked each group to try and find one word from the story that they would like to learn more about. She told her students that the word could be a word that they did not understand very well, a word that they think they needed to know, or a word they were curious to know more about. The most important thing to remember, Ms. Tan emphasized, was for each group to nominate a word, define the word by looking at how the author used it in the story, and tell the class why they thought it was important that the class learned the word. Some groups came up with a number of words, and Ms. Tan said that was all right because different groups might nominate the same words for the class vocabulary list. After allowing students about 5 minutes to discuss their nominations, Ms. Tan asked representatives from each group to share with the class the words they chose. She wrote each word on an overhead transparency and asked the class to define each word. She also asked students to share whatever they knew about the word. When she asked students to defend why they chose a word, they discussed why their word was important to know. Once the entire class had shared their words, definitions, and rationales, Ms. Tan rewrote the key vocabulary words on the chalkboard with the definitions decided by the class. She passed out VSS sheets and asked students to copy the words and definitions from the class list on the overhead (see Figure 20.2). Ms. Tan informed the class that they could refer to their new words when they wrote stories later in the day. She also told the class that she would include their vocabulary list in future word finds and word jumbles.

GRADE 1 HISTORY–SOCIAL SCIENCE GOALS

After unit lesson, students will be able to:

1. Understand the elements of fair play and good sportsmanship.
2. Show respect for the rights and opinions of others.
3. Understand the importance of respect for rules by which we live.
4. Recognize the ways in which they are all part of the same community, sharing principles, goals, and traditions despite their varied ancestry.

FIGURE 20.1. Goals for Ms. Tan's unit on citizenship.

Word	Student Definition	Rationale
canine	dog	"The police have K-9 units. Those are the cops with dogs."
prison	jail	"A prison is where you go when you are bad and can't get along with other people so they put you alone by yourself."
discussed	said; talked about	"We're discussing now!"
prevented	stopped	"When you prevent something it means you stop it from happening. That's why they say not to have fires in the forest because they can cause bigger fires . . . so you can prevent big fires by not making little fires."
refused	say "no"; won't do	"It's like when Munro (another story students read) told his parents he wouldn't take a bath or eat his dinner. He refused to."
shocking	surprise	"Something shocks you when you don't know it's going to happen."

FIGURE 20.2. Example of a vocabulary self-collection strategy. Ms. Tan asks students to double-check their definitions by comparing them with definitions found in their dictionaries. She does not write students' rationale for choosing a word on the chalkboard or on an overhead transparency. Rather, she asks students to tell her why they chose a word. It is written here to demonstrate how students feel about certain words.

References

Haggard, M. R. (1986). The vocabulary self-collection strategy: An active approach to word learning. In E. K. Dishner, T. W. Bean, J. E. Readence, & D. W. Moore (Eds.), *Reading in the content areas: Improving classroom instruction* (pp. 179–183). Dubuque, IA: Kendall/Hunt.

Readence, J. E., Bean, T. W., & Baldwin, R. S. (2001). *Content area literacy: An integrated approach* (7th ed.). Dubuque, IA: Kendall/Hunt.

Ruddell, M. R. (1992). Integrated content and long term vocabulary learning with the vocabulary self-collection strategy. In E. K. Dishner, T. W. Bean, J. E. Readence, & D. W. Moore (Eds.), *Reading in the content areas: Improving classroom instruction* (pp. 190–196). Dubuque, IA: Kendall/Hunt.

Text Resources

Carlson, N. L. (1988). *I like me!* New York: Viking Press.

Finchler, J., & O'Malley, K. (2002). *You're a good sport, Miss Malarkey.* New York: Walker.

James, V. J., & Strock, J. (2002). *Koala Kan learns about respect.* New York: Pentland Press.

Joslin, S., & Sendak, M. (1958). *What do you say, dear?* New York: HarperCollins.

Rubel, N. (2003). *Grody's not so golden rules.* New York: Silver Whistle.

Teague, M. (2002). *Dear Mrs. LaRue: Letters from obedience school.* New York: Scholastic.

Website Resources

Congress For Kids
congressforkids.net/citizenship_intro.htm

FirstGov for Kids
www.kids.gov

Good Citizenship: The Purpose of Education, by Eleanor Roosevelt
newdeal.feri.org/er/er19.htm

Vocabulary Self-Collection Strategy

Word	Student definition	Rationale

WORD PLAY:
Top Ten Lists

Lee Jung Su teaches fifth grade and was bored teaching students vocabulary words with lists and quizzes. A big fan of David Letterman's nightly Top Ten Lists (Letterman, 1990), Mr. Su began distributing a list every day to the students in his class. He asked students to get in pairs and small groups to change one word in each top ten list entry. Here is an example of what his students came up with:

"Top Ten Signs Your Kid's School Is Too Congested"

(The list was originally the "Top Ten Signs Your Kid's School Is Overcrowded," but Mr. Su's students replaced the word *overcrowded* with *congested*. For each "top ten" entry, students changed a word with a synonym.)

10. Kid comes home *exuberant* saying, "I got to ride inside the bus today!" (Students changed the word *excited* to *exuberant*.)

9. Principal sends *ultimatum*—he's not skipping class enough.

8. Teacher needs a U-Haul to *transport* home the book reports.

7. Losing 60 to 70 kids on class trip is considered *successful*.

6. School play is "The Ten Commandments"—*sufficient* students to play all 100,000 Hebrews.

5. Class photo is taken using government weather *satellite*.

4. The teacher *announces*, "Gus Van Rauschenbach," and 17 kids say, "Here."

3. Last spring's school bake sale *garnered* one and a quarter million.

2. There's a waiting list to get *tormented* by the school bully.

1. The kids actually *outnumber* the rodents.

I'd like to make a couple more points about this activity. First, students of all ages can play this game. I have seen fifth-grade teachers send students down to first-grade classrooms to help first graders think of words. Second, and more important, the reason I like this activity so much is that it makes the teacher, Lee Jung Su, smile every day. Teachers need to return the "fun" into their classrooms, as we are losing too many teachers who are burnt out in their "race to cheat to the top" so that "no child is left untested."

TEXT RESOURCE

Letterman, D. (1990). *The "Late Night with David Letterman" book of top ten lists.* New York: Pocket Books.

Vocab-o-grams

What Is It?

Vocab-O-Grams (Barr & Johnson, 1997; Blachowicz & Fisher, 2002), also known as "Predict-O-Grams," allow students to make predictions about how authors use particular words to tell a story. Vocab-o-grams are used with a charting process that asks students to organize vocabulary in relationship to the structure of the selection.

Why Is It Used?

This strategy is used to (1) allow students to go beyond the definition of a word and consider its application in text, and (2) encourage students to form predictions about a selection based on vocabulary words.

What Do I Do?

1 Using the chalkboard or an overhead transparency, write a list of new vocabulary words from the text that reflects the story structure.

2 As a whole class, discuss the meanings of the new vocabulary words. Distribute copies of story elements to the students (vocab-o-grams; see Figure 21.2 below).

3 Place students into small groups of three or four. Ask each group to use their knowledge of the new vocabulary words and story structure (setting, characters, problem/goal, actions, and resolution) to predict each word's use in the story. Tell students they may place a word under more than one category. If students have no clues about where a word should go, tell them to place the word in the "mystery words" section.

4 As a whole class, discuss where student groups placed vocabulary words. Words may be placed in more than one category. Elicit student knowledge about words and what strategies they employed to predict meanings.

5 Ask students to make predictions.

6 Ask each student to formulate a personal question to answer. Allow students to read text to confirm and reject their predictions.

7 After reading, discuss how the author employed the vocabulary words in the story.

How Do I Differentiate It?

Students enjoy predicting how they think stories are going to turn out, and vocab-o-grams allow students not only to predict what they think is going to happen in a story but which words to focus on as well. Teachers comment that the strength in vocab-o-grams seems to be in allowing students to work in pairs or small groups to test their different predictions with peers before sharing them with the entire class. Sal Parker asks his sixth graders to come up with different ways to present their vocab-o-grams to the entire class. For example, Mr. Parker's students have created skits, facilitated talk shows, performed puppet shows, shot short videos, and even created their own WebQuests.

Example

Deron McGinnis planned to read the West African folktale *Why Mosquitoes Buzz in People's Ears* (Aardema, Dillon, & Dillon, 1975) to his third graders. (The unit goals are shown in Figure 21.1.) He knew that many of the words in the story would be new to his students, so he chose a list of new vocabulary words for the class to review before reading the story. He wrote the list on an overhead transparency and asked students to discuss what they knew about the words. Next, he passed out vocab-o-gram handouts to the class (see Figure 21.2). Mr. McGinnis organized students into groups of four and asked each group to predict where each vocabulary word could be found as it related to the story structure. As an example, he asked students to place the word *village* in the most appropriate category. A group answered "setting," and Mr. McGinnis then asked students to think of a prediction they could make about a story with the word *village*. A student predicted that such a story would take place in a small town. Mr. McGinnis told students that they would be reading *Why Mosquitoes Buzz in People's Ears*, and they had to guess where their

---

GRADE 3 LANGUAGE ARTS GOALS

After unit lesson, students will be able to:

1. Ask questions and support answers by connecting prior knowledge with literal information found in, and inferred from, the text.
2. Demonstrate comprehension by identifying answers in the text.
3. Recall major points in the text and make and modify predictions about forthcoming information.
4. Distinguish the main idea and supporting details in expository text.
5. Extract appropriate and significant information from the text, including problems and solutions.

FIGURE 21.1. Goals for Mr. McGinnis's unit on story reading.

Story Title: "Why Mosquitoes Buzz in People's Ears"	
New vocabulary words:	
• alarmed • burrow • council • farmer • whining • feared • gathered • iguana • killed • mosquito • plotting • reeds • sticks	
Setting *farmer*	**Which words tell you about when and where the story took place?** *On a farm*
Characters *burrow farmer iguana mosquito*	**Which words tell you about the characters in the story (their feelings, thoughts, appearance)?** *There's a donkey and an iguana and a mosquito on a farm.*
Problem/goal *alarmed whining killed*	**Which words describe the problem or goal?** *One of the animals pulls a fire alarm because one animal was whining about mosquitoes biting him and he wants to kill it.*
Action *whining feared killed reeds*	**Which words tell you what might happen?** *The animals fear the farmer because they know if they are loud he will be mad. So when the mosquitoes come and they make noise, the farmer comes and kills the mosquitoes.*
Resolution *sticks*	**Which words tell you how the story might end?** *Maybe the farmer uses sticks to swat the mosquitoes off the animals.*
What question(s) do you have?	*Why don't the animals kill the mosquitoes? Why do mosquitoes buzz in people's ears?*
Mystery words: *council, plotting*	

FIGURE 21.2. Example of a vocab-o-gram.

new vocabulary words fit in the story (characters, setting, problem/goal, action, or resolution). If a group could not decide in which category to place a word, they could place the word in the "mystery word" category. Students worked in groups for about 10 minutes, placing words in categories and making predictions about the story. Mr. McGinnis asked groups to share their predictions and to explain how they came up with them, and then he asked each student to write at least one question about the story, based on previous predictions. He read aloud the story and discussed with students whether their predictions were accurate. Students shared their thoughts about the story and about different ways the author used the words.

References

Barr, R., & Johnson, B. (1997). *Teaching reading and writing in elementary classrooms* (2nd ed.). New York: Longman.

Blachowicz, C., & Fisher, P. J. (2002). *Teaching vocabulary in all classrooms* (2nd ed.). Upper Saddle River, NJ: Merrill/Prentice Hall.

Text Resources

Aardema, V., Dillon, L., & Dillon, D. (1975). *Why mosquitoes buzz in people's ears.* New York: Puffin Pied Piper.

Friedman, A., & Guevara, S. (1995). *A cloak for the dreamer.* New York: Scholastic.

Martin, R., & Shannon, D. (1998). *The rough-face girl.* New York: Paper Star.

Sendak, M. (1963). *Where the wild things are.* New York: HarperTrophy.

Thompson, K., & Knight, H. (1955). New York: Simon & Schuster.

Viorst, J., & Cruz. R. (1987). *Alexander and the terrible, horrible, no good very bad day.* New York: Aladdin.

Website Resources

E-Themes on Story Elements
Ethemes.missouri.edu/themes/607

Story Elements Games
learner.org/interactives/story

Story Generator
worsleyschool.net/socialarts/generate/astory.html

Vocab-o-gram

Story title:	
New vocabulary words:	
Setting	Which words tell you about when and where the story took place?
Characters	Which words tell you about the characters in the story (their feelings, thoughts, appearance)?
Problem/goal	Which words describe the problem or goal?
Action	Which words tell you what might happen?
Resolution	Which words tell you how the story might end?
What question(s) do you have?	
Mystery words:	

Vocabulary Cards
(Example/Nonexample)

What Is It?

Vocabulary cards (Frayer, Frederick, & Klausmeier, 1969; Tierney, Readence, & Dishner, 1995), also known as the Frayer Model, are used as a word-categorization activity that allows students to analyze a word by defining its essential and nonessential characterizations as well as provide examples and nonexamples. Students use an organizer divided into four squares to help complete the word analysis.

Why Is It Used?

The strategy is used to (1) allow students to analyze a word's essential and nonessential characteristics, (2) refine students' understanding of a concept or word by choosing examples and nonexamples, and (3) help students understand concepts by studying them in a relational manner.

What Do I Do?

1 Choose a text.

2 From the text, choose a word or concept to be analyzed. Write it in the center of a blank vocabulary card on the chalkboard or on an overhead transparency for the entire class to see.

3 Explain each of the four square components of the vocabulary card to students. Discuss how the vocabulary cards can be used as a graphic organizer.

4 Hand out blank vocabulary cards to the class (see Figure 22.2 below). Ask students to work with partners to complete the vocabulary card for the word or concept to be analyzed.

5 Once students have completed their vocabulary cards, ask them to share their ideas as a whole class. Using the chalkboard or the overhead projector, record student suggestions onto a class version of their vocabulary card.

How Do I Differentiate It?

Students enjoy creating vocabulary cards because the cards lend themselves to all sorts of variations. Students do not have to be concerned about "getting it right," as their cards can be examples of different concepts as well as nonexamples. Janet Wang says she learned vocabulary words when she was a little girl by playing with flash cards, and she enjoys letting her students create vocabulary cards because they think of their own ways to relate words to one another. She also uses the vocabulary cards as a way to help students understand the sequence of events in a story, as many of them appreciate the pictures and relate the pictures to the new target vocabulary words.

Example

Inez Sekakuku's first graders were beginning a unit on distinguishing different classes of animals: reptiles, amphibians, mammals, birds, fish, and anthropods. On the first day of the unit, Ms. Sekakuku told the class that they would be studying "mammals." (The unit goals are shown in Figure 22.1.) She wrote the word *mammals* in the center of a blank vocabulary card overhead. She briefly discussed with the class each of the vocabulary card's four squares: definition, characteristics, examples, and nonexamples (see Figure 22.2). Ms. Sekakuku asked students to find

---

GRADE 1 SCIENCE GOALS

After unit lesson, students will be able to:

1. Recognize that mammals are a class of animal.
2. Determine that mammals have certain traits that distinguish them from animals in other classes, such as fish, reptiles, and amphibians.
3. Acknowledge that there are many different types of mammals.
4. Understand that mammals are classified by two shared characteristics. They all feed their young with mammary gland milk and all have hair.

FIGURE 22.1. Goals for Ms. Sekakuku's unit on mammals.

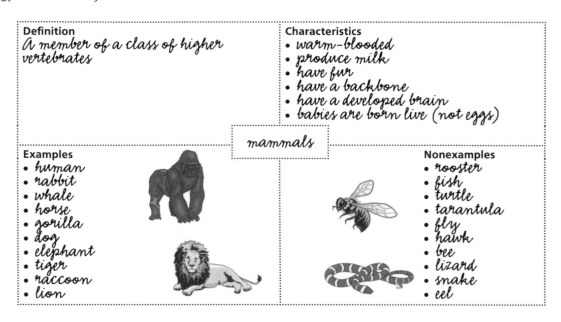

Definition
A member of a class of higher vertebrates

Characteristics
• warm-blooded
• produce milk
• have fur
• have a backbone
• have a developed brain
• babies are born live (not eggs)

mammals

Examples
• human
• rabbit
• whale
• horse
• gorilla
• dog
• elephant
• tiger
• raccoon
• lion

Nonexamples
• rooster
• fish
• turtle
• tarantula
• fly
• hawk
• bee
• lizard
• snake
• eel

FIGURE 22.2. Example of a vocabulary card on mammals.

partners and fill out their own vocabulary cards and be prepared to share with the rest of the class. After 15 minutes of paired work, students shared their vocabulary cards while Ms. Sekakuku recorded their responses on a class vocabulary card. Ms. Sekakuku told students that they would be creating vocabulary cards for each class of animals.

References

Frayer, D., Frederick, W. C., & Klausmeier, H. J. (1969). *A schema for testing the level of cognitive mastery.* Madison: Wisconsin Center for Education Research.

Tierney, R. J., Readence, J. E., & Dishner, E. K. (1995). *Reading strategies and practices: A compendium* (4th ed.). Boston: Allyn & Bacon.

Text Resources

Bruce, J. (2002). *Mammals: Explore and discover.* New York: Larousse Kingfisher Chambers.

Creagh, C. (1996). *Mammals.* New York: Time-Life Books.

Farrand, J., & Audubon Society. (1988). *Familiar mammals North America (Audubon Society Pocket Guides).* New York: Knopf.

McCourt, L., & Nathan, C. (2000). *Hairy 'n' weird.* Boston: Lowell House.

Snedden, R. (2002). *What is a mammal?* London: Gibbs Smith.

Young, J. (1990). *Amazing mammals.* New York: Knopf.

Website Resources

Animal Classes
www.kidzone.ws/animals/animal_classes.htm

KidsCom Animals of the World.
www.kidscom.com/games/animal/animal.html

National Geographic Animals and Nature
www.animalsnationalgeographic.com

Vocabulary Card

Definition	Characteristics

_____
Key word/concept

Examples	Nonexamples

WORD PLAY:
Palindromes

A palindrome is a word or phrase that can be read the same way, forward or backward. Ask students to think of palindromes or create new ones on their own. Here are some examples, including some palindromes created by students:

A man, a plan, a canal: Panama

Dad

Kayak

Level

Mom

Never odd or even

Race car

Radar

Rise to vote, sir.

Yo, Banana Boy!

TEXT RESOURCES

Agee, J. (2002). *Palindromania*. New York: Farrar, Straus and Giroux.
Miller, A. (1997). *Mad Amadeus sued a madam*. Boston: David R. Godine.
Terban, M. (1985). *Too hot to hoot: Funny palindrome riddles*. London: Sandpiper.

WEBSITE RESOURCES

Fun with Words
www.fun-with-words.com/palindromes.html

Fun-with-words.com is dedicated to amusing quirks, peculiarities, and oddities of the English language: word play. Playing with words and language is both entertaining and educational. This site offers a number of great word games, including plenty of engaging and entertaining palindromes.

Page O' Palindromes
www.megaera.org/palindromes.html

Includes several palindromes.

Word Plays

What Is It?

Word plays (Blachowicz & Fisher, 2002; Duffelmeyer, 1980) are an instructional strategy that utilizes dramatization to encourage students' vocabulary development. Using a short list of new vocabulary words or concepts, small groups of students create vignettes that feature and demonstrate the new vocabulary words or concepts.

Why Is It Used?

The strategy is used to (1) motivate students to make predictions about the possible use of words in a new text, (2) allow students to experiment with using words in their own speech, and (3) provide students with the opportunity to collaborate and discuss various meanings of new vocabulary words and concepts.

What Do I Do?

1 From a text, select three to five words that give an impression of the story structure (setting, characters, problem/goal, actions, and resolution). Write the words on index cards, and make sets of the cards for all student groups.

2 Give each group a set of cards (make sure that multiple groups receive the same words), and tell students to create a 3-minute skit based on the vocabulary.

3 Allow students to work in small groups and check for understanding as groups plan their skits.

4 Ask students to present their skits. Allow them to compare and contrast similarities and differences between their skits.

5 Ask students to read the text and compare the author's use of the vocabulary words with the way students used the words in their skits.

6 Ask students to highlight the vocabulary words when they encounter them in the text. After reading, ask students to take another look at the vocabulary words and clarify their meanings as the author intended.

7 Encourage students to use the new vocabulary words in other oral and written presentations.

How Do I Differentiate It?

In the example below Ed Polamalu gives his fifth graders 20 minutes to create an improvisational "word play" that uses the new vocabulary words that they have been given. While that works for Mr. Polamalu, observations of numerous classrooms has proven that it may be wiser to allow students only 5 to 7 minutes to create a skit. By giving students less time, teachers encourage all students in small groups to participate because they view the activity as an opportunity to "get silly." However, it has been observed that when students are given more time, the "thespians" of the group tend to take charge, while the more reserved group members stand on the margins. The point of word plays is not for students to come up with amazing skits; word plays are meant as a fun activity to encourage students to "think on their toes" and integrate new vocabulary words into everyday conversations.

Example

As part of a unit celebrating the diversity of cultures in America, Mr. Polamalu selected a number of texts for his fifth graders to read that chronicled the contributions of many important African Americans. (The unit goals are shown in Figure 23.1.) Today, he told his students, they would be creating short skits based on vocabulary words from the book *I Have a Dream* (King & Bryan, 1997), based on Martin Luther King, Jr.'s historic speech. Mr. Polamalu told the class that they would be performing word plays for each book they read. For this first word play, he told students, he was giving each small group of students the same five new vocabulary words that could be found in the book (*Negro, discrimination, civil rights, destiny,* and *brotherhood*). He told his students that he would give them 20 minutes to try to create a 3-minute skit that used all five words. They could be as creative as they wanted, he assured them, but they had to use the words correctly. They presented their skits, and students discussed the similarities and differences of their performances. Mr. Polamalu asked students to read the book in pairs and

---

GRADE 5 LANGUAGE PERFORMING ARTS GOALS

After unit lesson, students will be able to:

1. Use theatrical skills to dramatize events and concepts from other curriculum areas, such as reenacting the signing of the Declaration of Independence in history/social science.
2. Participate in improvisational activities to explore complex ideas and universal themes in literature and life.
3. Establish a situation, plot, point of view, and setting with descriptive words and phrases.
4. Show, rather than tell, the listener what happens.
5. Establish a controlling idea or topic.

FIGURE 23.1. Goals for Mr. Polamalu's unit on diversity.

highlight the parts of the text that used the new vocabulary words. After reading the text and discussing it with their partners, students shared their opinions as a class and discussed the similarities and differences between the text and their skits. Mr. Polamalu encouraged students to use the new vocabulary words in future oral and written presentations as they continued to celebrate Black History Month.

References

Blachowicz, C., & Fisher, P. J. (2002). *Teaching vocabulary in all classrooms* (2nd ed.). Upper Saddle River, NJ: Merrill/Prentice Hall.

Duffelmeyer, F. A. (1980). The influence of experience-based vocabulary instruction on learning word meanings. *Journal of Reading, 24,* 35–40.

Text Resources

Curtis, G., & Lewis, E. B. (1998). *The bat boy and his violin.* New York: Simon & Schuster.

Hopkinson, D., & Ransome, J. (1993). *Sweet Clara and the freedom quilt.* New York: Knopf.

King Jr., M. L. K., & Bryan, A. (1997). *I have a dream.* New York: Scholastic.

Pinkney, A. D. (1998). *Duke Ellington: The piano prince and his orchestra.* New York: Hyperion Press.

Rappaport, D., & Collier, B. (2000). *Freedom river.* New York: Hyperion Press.

Rappaport, D., & Collier, B. (2001). *Martin's big words: The life of Dr. Martin Luther King, Jr.* New York: Jump at the Sun.

Rockwell, A., & Christie, R. G. (2000). *Only passing through: The story of Sojourner Truth.* New York: Random House.

Website Resources

African American History & Heritage Site
creativefolk.com/blackhistory/blackhistory.html

Black History Month
www.infoplease.com/spot/bhm1.html

The Encyclopedia Britannica Guide to Black History
Britannica.com/blackhistory

Professor Garfield's Comics Lab
professorgarfield.org/pgf_comics_lab.html

Word Riddles

What Is It?

Word riddles (Blachowicz & Fisher, 2002; Gunning, 1996) are questions with pun-like responses. This instructional strategy arouses student interest in experimenting with different word uses, meanings, and structures. It is often used as an extension activity to encourage students to think about language beyond the classroom.

Why Is It Used?

The strategy is used to (1) build students' interest in word learning, (2) expand students' knowledge of homonyms and multiple meanings of words, and (3) provide students practice with common figures of speech.

What Do I Do?

1 From a text, choose a key concept (e.g., "space"), and ask students to brainstorm a list of words (e.g., *solar system, sun, moon, star, earth*) related to the key concept.

2 Select a word from the list (e.g., *star*).

3 Drop the first letter(s) from the word to get a shortened version (*star - s = tar*) and ask students to brainstorm a list of words that begin the way the shortened version begins (e.g., *target, tarantula, tartar sauce, tardy, Tarzan, tarp*).

4 Select a word from this list of words and put back the first letter that was initially dropped (e.g., *stardy, starget, Starzan*). This new "word" will serve as the answer to a riddle.

5 As a whole class, create a riddle question that highlights this word as an answer (e.g., What do you call a man who swings from planet to planet? "Starzan.").

6 Ask students to read a text and find more words to use for riddles (or select two to five additional key words from the text). Encourage students to work with partners and create riddles on their own.

7 Share riddles as a whole class.

How Do I Differentiate It?

While most strategies offered in this book can be adapted to meet the needs of students of any age, word riddles really work only for students up until the middle of third grade. Ask your eighth graders to create catchy word riddles, and you may just have a revolt on your hands. For younger students, though, word riddles can be a lot of fun, as they offer students a way to exhibit their developing sense of humor. Based on personal experience and the feedback of countless teachers, however, teachers need to be warned that the moment they begin to encourage their students to create riddles, many students (especially young boys) will insist on telling riddles every day. Many boys choose to tell the same riddle every day, and every day their riddle has a new punch line . . . and every day that punch line is not funny. In other words, word riddles are not for the "weak-of-heart" teacher.

Example

Eva Erikkson's first graders were studying space. (The unit goals are shown in Figure 24.1.) They had created papier mâché models of the Sun, Earth, and Moon; they had sung songs about the Earth; and they had studied how the Sun warms the Earth.

GRADE 1 SCIENCE GOALS

After unit lesson, students will be able to:

1. Explain how the sun applies heat and light to the earth.
2. Describe how night and day are caused by the rotation of the earth.
3. Explain that the sun is the source of heat and light that warms the land, air, and water.
4. Describe what can be observed in the sky by the unaided eye in the day and at night (e.g., sun, moon, stars).
5. Observe and identify the basic components of the solar system (e.g., sun, planets).
6. Observe stars in relation to the earth and the universe (e.g., number, brightness, basic constellations).

FIGURE 24.1. Goals for Mrs. Erikkson's unit on space.

> **Key concept:** space
>
> **Words related to key concept:** sun, moon, earth, asteroids, Mars, galaxy, universe, solar system, star, meteor
>
> **Key word:** star
>
> **Key word - first letter:** tar
>
> **Words that start with** *tar*: tarantula, tarp, target, Tarzan, tartar sauce, tardy
>
> **New words:** starantula, starp, starget, Starzan, startar sauce, stardy
>
> **Riddles:**
>
> 1. What do you call a man who swings from planet to planet? Starzan.
> 2. What do you call a spider that lives in outer space? A starantula.
> 3. How do you get a bull's-eye in space? Aim at the starget.
> 4. What do you put on a fish sandwich in outer space? Startar sauce.
> 5. What do you call it when the sun comes up late? The sun is stardy.

FIGURE 24.2. Examples of word riddles created by students.

Today, Mrs. Erikkson was reading a passage from the book *The Stars: A New Way to See Them* (Rey, 1976), to the class. In language arts she had been practicing riddles with her students, and they loved playing with words. So Mrs. Erikkson told the class that they were going to create riddles about outer space and make a class book to share with their parents. She asked her excited students to brainstorm words that they had heard as they had talked about outer space. After creating a short list, Mrs. Erikkson chose the word *star* and asked her students to drop the initial sound. She wrote the word *tar* on the chalkboard and asked her students to think of words that started with *tar*. After the class brainstormed some words and inserted the letter *s* at the beginning, she asked students to work with partners and try to think of riddles for their new words (see Figure 24.2). Students shared their riddles as a class, and then Mrs. Erikkson asked her students to continue to work with their partners and think of riddles with another key word they had discussed (*earth*). She told the class that they would create a riddle book with all of their riddles.

References

Blachowicz, C., & Fisher, P. J. (2002). *Teaching vocabulary in all classrooms* (2nd ed.). Upper Saddle River, NJ: Merrill/Prentice Hall.

Gunning, T. G. (1996). *Creating reading instruction for all children* (2nd ed.). Boston: Allyn & Bacon.

Text Resources

Dayrell, E., & Lent, B. (1968). *Why the sun and the moon live in the sky*. Boston: Houghton Mifflin.

Gibbons, G. (1999). *Stargazers*. New York: Holiday House.

Hort, L., & Ransome, J. E. (1997). *How many stars in the sky?* New York: Mulberry Books.

Lee, F. (2001). *Wishing on a star: Constellation stories and stargazing activities for kids*. Layton, UT: Gibbs Smith.

Oughton, J., & Desmini, L. (1996). *How the stars fell into the sky: A Navajo legend*. Boston: Houghton Mifflin.

Rey, H. A. (1976). *The stars: A new way to see them*. New York: Mariner Books.

Website Resources

Compound Word Riddles
www.rickwalton.com/curricul/wcomprid.htm

Hubble Space Telescope
hubblesite.org

NASA Space Link
nasa.gov/audience/forstudents/index.html

Sky and Telescope
skyandtelescope.com

Word Riddles
www.justriddlesandmore.com/wriddles.html

Word Riddles

1. Key concept:

_____

2. Words related to key concept:

_____

_____

_____

3. Key word to start with:

_____

4. Key word minus first letter(s):

_____

5. Words that begin with letters in number 4:

_____

_____

_____

6. Riddles:

_____

_____

_____

_____

_____

_____

_____

_____

_____

_____

_____

_____

Word Sorts

What Is It?

Word sorts (Bear, Invernizzi, Templeton, & Johnston, 1996; Cunningham, Moore, Cunningham, & Moore, 1995; Gunning, 2003) is an instructional strategy used to help students see the generative nature of words. Students "sort" words written and chosen by the teacher on individual cards into groups based on commonalities, relationships, and/or other criteria.

Why Is It Used?

The strategy is used to (1) assist students in learning the relationships among words and how to categorize words based on those relationships, (2) activate and build on students' prior knowledge of words, and (3) allow students to understand recurring patterns in words (e.g., rhyming words, number of syllables).

What Do I Do?

1 Select 5 to 10 words (more words for older students) from the text that relate to key concepts you want students to understand.

2 In addition, select any other difficult words from the passage that students will need to understand in order to comprehend the passage.

3 Select some words that will help the existing words fit into categories.

4 Print the words on a sheet of paper and make enough copies for all students in class. Allow students to cut out word "cards" for themselves.

5 From your list of words, present categories for students to use as they sort ("closed sort"), or ask students to select categories for sorting their words ("open sort").

6 Have students work in pairs or in small groups. Ask students to discuss and categorize their word cards by taping their cards under appropriate categories on a piece of butcher paper.

7 Ask students to share their categories with the whole class and explain their rationale for placing words in different categories.

8 Allow students to revise their word sorts after the group discussion.

How Do I Differentiate It?

Word sorts allow students to classify groups of words as they see fit. It is one of the favorite vocabulary activities offered by many teachers, especially early elementary school teachers. Pat Thompson, a second-grade teacher, says that she uses word sorts with her students as a way of seeing how their minds operate. "I use it as an assessment, but not in the way some 'test-crazy' folks think," she says. "When my students sort their words, it allows me to ask them about their thought process . . . [which] helps me determine new ways to present information to certain students in ways that are meaningful to them." Like Thompson, many teachers use word sorts as a way of relating students' prior knowledge to new concepts, making target vocabulary words much more comprehensible to students.

Example

Tamiko Hiroshi's fourth graders were studying recycling. (The unit goals are shown in Figure 25.1.) She had introduced a variety of books to the class, and in her third day of the unit she selected a couple of passages from the book *Fifty Simple Things Kids Can Do to Save the Earth* (Earthworks Group & Montez, 1990). These passages continued to focus on the three R's she had been teaching her class: recycle, reuse, and reduce. Mrs. Hiroshi selected words from the passages that she believed were unfamiliar to most of her students. As a number of words contained similar prefixes, she asked students to work in pairs to categorize each word based on its prefix (closed sort). Knowing that this would be a fairly simple activity for her fourth graders, Mrs. Hiroshi then asked them to create their own categories for words as well (open sort). After students completed both the closed sort and the open sort, Mrs. Hiroshi asked them to share their work with the class (see Figure 25.2). Students explained why they placed words in various categories for the closed sort, and they told the class why they had created the categories they had for the open sort. Mrs. Hiroshi allowed students to make any changes they deemed necessary for their final word sorts.

GRADE 4 SCIENCE GOALS

After unit lesson, students will be able to:

1. Comprehend the environmental issues our planet faces.
2. Become familiar with popular attitudes toward recycling and the practice of recycling in the community.
3. Determine whether a given resource is renewable or nonrenewable, and identify products they use that come from some natural resources.
4. Describe the impact of human activities on different natural resources, and develop an understanding for the need to conserve and preserve the earth's treasures.

FIGURE 25.1. Goals for Mrs. Hiroshi's unit on recycling.

Closed Sort (teacher-created categories)

Prefixes

con-	dis-	re-
conservation	disappear	recycle
contemplate	disintegrate	reduce
consume	disabled	respect
construct	disaster	reusable
container	distance	responsibility
consider	discover	resource

Open Sort (two student-created categories)

Syllables

2-syllable words	3-syllable words	4-or-more-syllable words
consume	contemplate	conservation (4)
construct	container	disintegrate (4)
distance	consider	reusable (4)
reduce	disappear	responsibility (6)
respect	disabled	
resource	disaster	
	discover	
	recycle	

Parts of speech

Nouns	Verbs	Adjectives
conservation	contemplate	disabled
construct	consume	reusable
container	construct	
disaster	consider	
distance	disappear	
respect	disintegrate	
responsibility	discover	
resource	recycle	
	reduce	
	respect	

recycle	conservation	reduce
contemplate	disappear	consume
disintegrate	respect	construct
container	disabled	reusable
consider	disaster	resource
discover	responsibility	distance

FIGURE 25.2. Example of word sorts.

References

Bear, D. R., Invernizzi, M., Templeton, S., & Johnston, F. (1996). *Words their way: Word study for phonics, vocabulary, and spelling instruction.* Upper Saddle River, NJ: Merrill/Prentice Hall.

Cunningham, P. M., Moore, S. A., Cunningham, J. W., & Moore, D. W. (1995). *Reading and writing in elementary classrooms: Strategies and observations.* New York: Longman.

Gunning, T. G. (2003). *Creating reading instruction for all children* (4th ed.). Boston: Allyn & Bacon.

Text Resources

Earthworks Group, & Montez, M. (1990). *Fifty simple things kids can do to save the earth.* New York: Scott Foresman.

Madden, D. (1993). *The wartville wizard.* Hong Kong: Aladdin Library.

Paulson, R. P., & Gerdes, D. (1999). *Sir Johnny's recycling adventure.* Sparta, NJ: Crestmont.

Schwartz, L., & Armstrong, B. (1990). *Earth book for kids: Activities to help heal the environment.* Santa Barbara, CA: Learning Works.

Seuss, D. (1971). *The lorax.* New York: Random House.

Showers, P., & Chewning, R. (1994). *Where does the garbage go?* New York: Scott Foresman.

Website Resources

Environmental Explorers Club
www.epa.gov/kids/

Recycling for Kids
kidsrecycle.org

Word Sorting
www.starfall.com/

Index

[Page numbers in *italic* refer to figures.]

AAA Math Fractions, 29
AAA Math–Third Grade, 93
African American History &
    Heritage Site, 137
All About Fractions, 19
Analogies, 9–15
    differentiation, 10
    example of classroom
        instruction, 10–11
    instructional goals, 9, *10*
    resources for teachers, 11–12
    teaching technique, 9–10
    worksheets, *13–15*
Angel Fire Idiom Games, 47
Animal Classes, 131
AplusMath, 19, 82

B

Barrel Full of Words, 78
Barrier games, 16–19
    differentiation, 17
    example, 17–19
    instructional goals, 16, *18*
    procedure, 16–17
    resources for teaching, 19
Ben's Guide to Symbols of
    Government, 59
Black History Month, 137
Book Adventure Kids Zone, 115
BookPals Storyline, 85, 88, 115
Book talk, 89
Braingle, 32
Building Vocabulary with Journey
    North, 36

C

Categorization skills, 61
Compound Word Riddles, 141
Comprehension
    possible sentences strategy for,
        79–80
    semantic feature analysis for,
        94–95
    vocabulary knowledge and, 4

Concept ladders, 21–25
    differentiation, 22
    example, 22–23
    instructional goals, 21, *22*
    procedure, 21–22
    resources for teaching, 23–24
    worksheet, *25*
Congress for Kids, 120
Constitution Facts, 52
Context clues for learning word
    meaning
    implications for vocabulary
        instruction, 7
    limitations to, 3
    significance of, 3
    technique, 2
Contextual redefinition, 26–30
    differentiation, 27
    example, 27–29
    instructional goals, 26, 27
    procedure, 26–27
    resources for teaching, 29
    worksheet, *30*
Cool Math, 82

Cool Math 4 Kids, 19, 82, 109
CyberSleuth Kids, 36

D

Dino Base, 103
Dino Hunt, 103
Dinosauria, 103
Discovery School, 29
Dittograms, 78
Dr. Goodword's Vocabulary
     Games, 71

E

Encyclopedia Britannica Guide to
     Black History, 137
Environmental Explorers Club, 146
Eponyms, 43
Ethan's Oxymoron Page, 111
E-Themes on Story Elements, 126
Exclusion brainstorming, 33–37
     differentiation, 34
     example, 34–35
     instructional goals, 33, *35*
     procedure, 33–34
     resources for teaching, 35–36
     worksheet, *37*
Explorer Links, 12

F

Fern's Poetry Club, 76
FirstGov for Kids, 120
Food Idioms and Sayings, 47
Frayer Model, 128
Free Graphic Organizers, 103
Fun Brain Math, 82
Fun Brain Money Math, 19
Funny Poetry for Children, 76
Fun with Words, 32, 64, 133

G

Good Citizenship: The Purpose of
     Education, 120
Great American Landmarks
     Adventure, 59

H

Henry's Piksas Game, 29
Hierarchical and linear arrays,
     38–42
     differentiation, 39
     example, 39–40
     instructional goals, 38, *39*
     procedure, 38–39
     resources for teaching, 40–41
     worksheet, *42*
High school, 8
Hink pinks, *54*
History for Kids, 36
Hubble Space Telescope, 141
Human Body, The, 88

I

Idiom Connection, The, 47
Idioms, 44–48
     definition, 44
     instructional goals, 44, *46*
     instructional procedure, 44–47
     resources for teaching, 47
     worksheet, *48*
Instant Poetry Forms, 76
Interactive Units Converter, 93
Interactive word walls, 49–53
     differentiation, 50
     example, 50–52
     instructional goals, 49, *51*
     procedure, 49–50
     resources for teaching, 52
     worksheet, *53*

J

Jokes N Jokes, 66
Just Curious: Environmental
     Science, 97

K

KidsCom Animals of the World,
     131
Kids Mysteries, 24
Kids Online Resources, 12
Kids Web–Weather, 64

K–W–L plus, 55–60
     differentiation, 56
     example, 56–57, *58*
     instructional goals, 55, *57*
     procedure, 55–56
     resources for teaching, 59
     worksheet, *60*

L

Lazy Readers' Book Club, The, 89
Learning styles, 6
Linear arrays. *See* Hierarchical
     and linear arrays
Line Symmetry, 109
List–group–label, 61–65
     differentiation, 62
     example, 62–64
     instructional goals, 61, *63*
     procedure, 61–62
     resources for teaching, 64
     worksheet, *65*

M

Mathematical Morphemes, 71
Math Forum, K–12 Geometry,
     109
Math Is Fun, 82
Math Words, 71
Memorization
     traditional vocabulary building
         strategies, 4–5, 6
Middle school, 8
Mindjet, 103
Morphemic analysis, 67–72
     definition, 67
     differentiation, 68
     example, 69–71
     instructional goals, 67, *69*
     procedure, 67–68
     resources for teaching, 71
     worksheet, *72*

N

NASA Space Link, 141
National Geographic Animals
     and Nature, 131

National Geographic Expeditions, 97

National Historic Landmarks Program, 59

National Park Service, 59

Neologisms, 20

New word acquisition
  average rate per year of, 2
  basic principles of, 7
  context clues for, 2–3, 7
  diversity of learning styles for, 6
  meaningfulness of context in, 3
  number of exposures for, 3
  reading as method for, 4
  See also Vocabulary
    instruction; Vocabulary
    knowledge

November, Alan, 8

O

Online Children's Stories, 115

Oxymoron List, 111

Oxymorons, 111

P

Page O' Palindromes, 133

Paint by Idioms, 47

Palindromes, 133

Pangrams, 99

PBS Kids Between the Lions Read Aloud, 88

PBS Kids Between the Lions— Stories, 115

Personal vocabulary journals, 73–77
  definition, 73
  differentiation, 74
  example, 74–76
  instructional goals, 73, *75*
  resources for, 76
  use of, 73–74
  worksheet, *77*

Pictograms, 41

Poetry for Kids Links, 76

Possible sentences, 79–83
  differentiation, 80
  example, 80, *81*
  instructional goals, 79, *81*

procedure, 79–80
  resources for teaching, 82
  worksheet, *83*

Predict-o-grams, 123

Prefixes. *See* Morphemic analysis

Problem Site, The, 19

Professor Garfield's Comics Lab, 137

Puzzles
  rhyming riddles, *54*

Puzzle Soup, 32

Q

Quia Face Idioms, 47

Quia Vocab/Word Knowledge: Awesome Analogies, 12

Quiz-Tree Idioms, 47

QWERTY keyboard, 6

R

Readability of texts, 3

Read-alouds, 84–88
  differentiation, 85
  example, 86, *87*
  instructional goals, 84, *86*
  procedure, 84–85
  resources for teaching, 87–88
  weekly book talk, 89

Read Alouds: Trelease on Reading, 88

Readaquarium, 10, 12

Rebuses, 31–32

Rebus Puzzles, 41

Recycling for Kids, 146

Rhymes, in hink pink riddles, *54*

Riddles, *54,* 138–142

RinkWorks, 99

Roadmap to the U.S. Constitution, A, 52

Roman Empire, The, 36

S

Scavenger hunts, 90–93
  differentiation, 91
  example, 91–92
  instructional goals, 90, *92*

procedure, 90–91
  resources for teaching, 93

Scientific Method, The, 41

Semantic feature analysis, 94–98
  example, *95–96*
  instructional goals, 94, *96*
  procedure, 94–95
  resources for teaching, 97
  worksheet, *98*

Semantic mapping, 100–104
  definition, 100
  differentiation, 101
  example, 101, *102*
  instructional goals, 100, *102*
  procedure, 100–101
  resources, 103
  worksheet, *104*

Short-term memory, 6

Six Word Stories, 24

Sky and Telescope, 141

Sniglets, 20

Stone Soup magazine, 24

Story Element Games, 126

Story Generator, 126

Structural analysis, 26

Student VOC strategy, 105–110
  differentiation, 106
  example, 106–107, *108*
  instructional goals, 105, 107
  procedure, 105–106
  resources for teaching, 107, 109
  worksheet, *110*

Suffixes. *See* Morphemic analysis

T

Taking America's Measure, 93

Teaching the Scientific Method, 41

Technical vocabulary, 61

Text talk, 112–115
  differentiation, 113
  example, 113–114
  instructional goals, 112, *114*
  procedure, 112–113
  resources for teaching, 115

Text types, 84, 85

Thinks.com, 111

Tom Swifties, 66

Top Ten Lists, 122

tree diagrams, 38

Trelease's Read-Aloud Handbook, 115
Typewriter keyboard, 5–6

U

United States Geography Games, 97
U.S. National Archives and Records Administration, 52
U.S.A. Games, 97

V

Verbal ability
 significance of vocabulary knowledge in determining, 3
 use of list–group–label technique to enhance, 61
Visual Fractions, 29
Vocab-o-grams, 123–127
 differentiation, 124
 example, 124–126
 instructional goals, 123, *125*
 procedure, 123–124
 resources for teaching, 126
 worksheet, *127*
Vocabulary cards, 128–132
 differentiation, 129
 example of classroom use, 129–130
 instructional goals, 128, *129*
 resources for teaching, 130–131
 use of, 128–129
 worksheet, *132*
Vocabulary instruction
 basic principles of, 7
 diversity of learning styles and, 6
 exclusion brainstorming for, 33–34
 goals, 7
 morphemic analysis for, 67–68
 read-alouds for, 84–85
 scavenger hunt strategy for, 90–91

selection of words for, 7
semantic feature analysis for, 94–95
semantic mapping strategy for, 100–101
shortcomings of current approaches, 4
strategies for, 7–8
student VOC strategy for, 105–106
text talk strategy for, 112–113
traditional approaches to, 4–6
use of analogies for, 9–10
use of barrier games for, 16–17
use of concept ladders for, 21–22
use of contextual redefinition for, 26–27
use of idioms for, 44–45
use of interactive word walls for, 49–50
use of list–group–label technique for, 61–62
use of personal journals for, 73–74
vocab-o-gram strategy for, 123–124
vocabulary self-collection strategy for, 116–117
word plays for, 134–135
Vocabulary knowledge
 as predictor of verbal ability, 3
 as readability factor, 3
 See also New word acquisition; Vocabulary instruction
Vocabulary self-collection, 116–121
 differentiation, 117
 example, 118, *119*
 instructional goals, 116, *118*
 procedure, 116–117
 resources for, 119–120
 worksheet, *121*

W

Weather Dude, 64
Webquest.org, 93

Websites
 for analogies instruction, 12
 archives of dead links, 8
 barrier game resources, 19
 book talk resources, 89
 concept ladder resources, 24
 contextual redefinition resources, 29
 dittogram resources, 78
 eponym resources, 43
 exclusion brainstorming resources, 36
 for hierarchical and linear array instruction, 41
 idiomatic expression resources, 47
 interactive word wall resources, 52
 K–W–L plus resources, 59
 list–group–label resources, 64
 morphemic analysis resources, 71
 oxymoron lists, 111
 palindrome resources, 133
 pangram resource, 99
 personal vocabulary journal resources, 76
 for possible sentences strategy, 82
 read-aloud resources, 85, 88
 rebus resources, 32
 riddle resources, 141
 scavenger hunt resources, 91, 93
 for semantic feature analysis, 97
 semantic mapping resources, 103
 student VOC strategy resources, 109
 for text talk instruction, 115
 for Tom Swifties, 66
 vocabulary card resources, 131
 for vocabulary self-collection, 120
 for word and math puzzles, *54*
 word play resources, 137
 word sort resources, 146
Wegryn, Jim, 78

Wizards & Pigs, 76
Word plays, 134–137
  differentiation, 135
  example, 135–136
  instructional goals, 134, *136*
  procedure, 134–135
  resources for teaching,
    136–137
Word Problems for Kids, 82
Word riddles, 138–142
  definition, 138
  differentiation, 139
  example, 139–140

instructional goals, 138, *139*
  resources for teaching,
    140–141
  worksheet, *142*
Word Roots and Prefixes, 71
Word Sorting, 146
Word sorts, 143–146
  differentiation, 144
  example, 144, *145*
  instructional goals, 143, *145*
  procedure, 143–144
  resources for teaching, 146
Wordstorming, 62

Word walls. *See* Interactive word
  walls
Wuzzles & Puzzles, *54*

Y

Your Digestive System, 88

Z

Zgonc, Yvette, 4